Secrets of
Winning Fast Break
Basketball

Previous books by Burrall Paye:

Basketball's Zone Presses: A Complete Coaching Guide
Complete Coaching Guide to Basketball's Match-Up Zone

Previous book by Aubrey Bonham

Coaching the Flexible Man-to-Man Defense

SECRETS OF WINNING FAST BREAK BASKETBALL

Aubrey Bonham
with Burrall Paye

Parker Publishing Company, Inc.
West Nyack, New York

© 1984 by
Parker Publishing Company, Inc.

Library of Congress Cataloging in Publication Data

Bonham, Aubrey R.,
  Secrets of winning fast break basketoall.

  Includes index.
  1. Basketball—Coaching. 2. Basketball—Offense.
I. Paye, Burrall   II. Title.
GV885.3.B66 1984   796.323'077   84-6997
ISBN 0-13-798745-5

Printed in the United States of America

DEDICATION

This book is dedicated to my dear wife Margaret who was the greatest contributor to the book and my life.

HOW THIS BOOK
WILL HELP YOU DEVELOP
YOUR FAST BREAK

Do you think about getting the ball so you can score? Or do you think about getting the ball so you can prevent your opponent from scoring? These two questions are basic, but their answers determine your real philosophy on fast break basketball. The first reveals that you are not as interested in defense as getting the ball and going. This leads to hit-and-miss fast break basketball—what old coaches used to call the "plunge and thunder" fast break. The latter question is more fundamentally sound. It reveals a coach who will work at perfecting execution and smart team play in his fast break system.

With today's combination defenses, match-ups, switches every other possession, etc., it just makes good sense to get the shot before the defense can get set. Patterned-type ball clubs work hard against set defenses to get the same jump shot your fast break will get for you. The difference: the fast break offense gets the shot quicker with less opportunity for a turnover.

You can bring the ball into your offensive end by using one of four methods: a.) walk the ball downcourt with no semblance of a fast break, b.) run your primary break from which you change to your regular offense if the desired shot does not come from the fast break, c.) run your primary break into a quick-scoring secondary break that will go immediately into your half-court offense, or d.) run the ball to the offensive end to avoid back-court pressure and then convert to your regular offense.

All teams need the ability to play at each of these tempos; but each team needs to establish its best tempo if it is to win consistently. If your team can operate under set c.) above, it can operate under any of the four tempos. That is why *Secrets of Winning Fast Break Basketball*, which develops set c.) completely, is so very, very important to you.

Just as there are four ways to advance the ball into front court, there are four basic ways to begin your fast break. Your defense can gain a loose ball, intercept a pass, or steal a dribble. From there you explode into your fast break. This is the second most prevalent means of getting into a fast break. The most prevalent way is after a free-throw missed, after a field-goal missed, after a free-throw made, or after a field-goal made. You grab the defensive rebound, throw the outlet pass, fill the lanes, and score before your opponents can recover. Should your opponents make their field-goal attempt or free-throw attempt, your assigned player takes the ball out-of-bounds, throws it inbounds to your inbounds receiver, fills the lanes, and scores before your opponents realize you are attacking. And you do it with the same simple basic fast break pattern, making the maneuvers easy for your players to master. And this same pattern can be executed from jump ball situations and from side out-of-bounds plays when your opponents are pressuring you. Furthermore, the same pattern works when your team is facing a full-court man-to-man or zone press.

This basic simplicity alone is worth the price of the book. Even if your system is different from this one, the overview will certainly give you an idea of how to better organize your own fast break.

Chapter 1 underlines the teaching problems. It also points up the basic keys to a successful fast break offense. Chapter 2 covers the details for the development of defensive and offensive rebounds, which is the backbone of any fast break system. Your basic break begins with the rebound and the outlet pass and can continue until you tip-in the missed shot. In succeeding chapters the basic moves are emphasized, the variations are presented, and all the drills which you need to tutor your break are complete and in an orderly array. Fast break play against presses, zones, and special situations are introduced in Chapter 8. In fact, *Secrets of Winning Fast Break Basketball* carries you from the securing of the rebound to the outlet pass to the running of the lanes to the secondary phase into your half-court offense. And it all but guarantees you will score. Plus all of it is taught through fundamentally sound drills which improve your team's abilities daily. One single basic pattern, which is expanded and contracted with multiple options, is all you need to attack special situations, full-court presses, made and missed shots, sideline out-of-bounds under pressure, and jump balls. And there has never been a chapter on fast break basketball like Chapter 4. Its ideas, drills, and development will improve your offensive system even if ours does not meet your needs.

Aubrey Bonham
with Burrall Paye

CONTENTS

SECRETS OF ORGANIZING
YOUR FAST BREAK

1

Most fast-break coaching problems occur in the execution of the skills at a *high tempo*. Every player has a limit to his ability to break fast and yet retain the control necessary to employ his skills efficiently. Even one step too fast produces turnovers in passing, traveling, or offensive fouls. Fast break tempo and efficiency will improve throughout the season if the basics are mastered.

You must control the learning speed. You must slow it down when necessary, speed it up when you feel it is profitable. Your fast break goal is to organize and control ball movement. Your aim must be to gain a tempo above the ability of the opposition to slow it down.

You can accomplish this by keeping good control of your scrimmages. While scrimmaging, you must check each player's fast break skills. Your players' skills are the basis of any fast break future success. You should teach individual skill development throughout the season. The open play of any fast break system makes it imperative to concentrate on the skill development of each player, makes it necessary to put special emphasis on all the little details of each fast break position.

Why Play Fast Break Basketball?

The answer to defensive pressure is offensive pressure: attacking, always attacking. A fast break coach wants many options in the initial phase of his fast break; and he wants the initial phase to flow smoothly into a secondary phase. The fast break coach wants these options to occur in the lanes the players run, in passing one time and getting there by dribbling the next, in every conceivable manner. Although the fast break coach wants versatility and flexibility, he also wants simplicity.

Fast-break ball teams do not only want to outnumber the defense and score; they want to be able to execute the power play against the weakest point of the defense without any loss of motion or any hesitation. Good fast break teams can execute the fast-break power play even when the defense outnumbers the offense. They want to execute the power play when the defense is at its weakest—after the defense has stopped the first wave of the break but just before the defense has all five defenders properly positioned for their half-court defense. This phase is called the secondary break. But should the secondary break fail, you want to get into your half-court offense without having to reset.

By this smooth flow from primary break to secondary break to set offense, defensive players are forced to continuously consider two or more attack possibilities. The defense will never be allowed to reset, to regroup. The options and the variations in the fast break pattern will force the defense to hesitate, to consider its next move, and thus make its counter a step or two late.

The secret of continuous attack is smooth passing and lane changing as the break applies the final power thrust to score. You strike hard, while the defense is trying to cover its 1-on-1 assignments and position ball side or position for defensive help. The key: You do not give the defense time to form into a close-knit unit.

To develop a complete fast break system, your initial pattern must have simple options which can be executed at full speed. From this initial thrust, the pattern flows gently into a simple secondary break. From there, the flow continues into your basic half-court offense. This is your fast break system. It becomes a great fast break system when this pattern can be used to break the full-court presses, to inbounds the ball against pressure, to use in jump ball situations, and to attack even after your opponents score.

You must keep increased pressure on the defense with a mind set to attack! attack! attack! You must insure continuous momentum by eliminating break errors that might give the momentum back to your opponents. Continuous patterns prevent the defense from getting set, and thereby prevent further ball penetration.

Passing is one of the important keys to the success of any fast-break team offense. Your offensive success is in direct proportion to the amount of pass practice time you set aside in your daily plans. There seems to be two approaches to the fast break offense. One is a broad-based pattern with the passing skills almost sharpened to perfection. The other is one of many nonrelated single patterns with mediocre passing skills. If you let your squad get by with mediocre passing skills, do not expect them to improve much during the season. A sloppy habit is tough to break.

The next important skill to be developed by the passers to insure fast break success is the fake away from the passing lane you want opened. A fast fake will not move the defense from the passing lane. A good fake takes the defensive pressure away from the passing lane to be used. Passing is a key. The fake also insures a great deal more penetration. It eliminates many outside shots because the fake opens passing lanes into the 60 percent area. Drills presented throughout this book will develop passing, fake passing, and receiving while running at full speed. Drills presented while teaching the fast break also include shooting and gaining body control while moving at an up tempo.

Most coaches realize that missed shots can be traced to a lack of body control. The player who is forced to play at a higher tempo in order to get his shots off will miss them, turn the ball over, have a "bad night." Because he had to stop faster (with his body tensions not released) before going into his shot, he will more often than not miss it. He had poor stop balance. This results in poor air balance. Successful shooting of a jump shot at the end of a break depends on the ability to execute the one-count jump-stop with balance, with relaxation, and with concentration on good shot mechanics.

Fast break fundamental drills of passing, shooting, and body control will even help your half-court offense. Practicing at an up-tempo develops your players for the fast game and the slow game. But practicing at a slow tempo will never prepare your players for those nights when opposing defenses force you into a quicker game.

Fast break coaches can expect to win four or five games by outconditioning their opponents. If you can force your opposition to a tempo above their practice and game speed, their players will show a second and fourth quarter drop in execution and board play. Your fast break conditioning has your team ready to take advantage of their opponents' slow-down.

Some teams have a tendency to slow their attack momentum and pull back as the defense ahead of the ball gets tougher. But the continuation from fast break to secondary break to set offense keeps your attack moving toward the basket.

A consistent game-length fast break may need help from your bench. Your sixth, seventh, and eighth players should come close to the starting five. The extra guard, forward, and center, or the three guards and forwards, must keep the pressure on. This helps develop team morale, team commitment. Your practices improve in intensity and development. It is also insurance against fouls, sickness, bad nights, or the loss of a player because of poor grades.

How to Analyze Your Squad's Fast Break Potential

You must first make an individual analysis of your squad. You rate them on a scale of one to ten for each fast break skill: rebound ability, inside-outside passing, speed, dribbling with pass-offs, experience, balance, and learning readiness.

After you rate your players, you should still be prepared for some surprises. A lower-rated player, after two or three weeks of practice, may develop faster than you originally expected. But a well-organized rating system will pay dividends in the long run.

The most important decision of the year confronts the coach when he chooses his starting five along with alternates at guard, wing, and center. Some coaches make frequent changes during the first half of the season. That can cost you a winning season. Do not put off choosing your starting five.

Sometimes you may choose a player who has less comparative individual skill. You choose him because his kind of play contributes to a team's cohesiveness that insures solid team play. Your squad should have some underclassmen who can hand down the break offense. This will start a fast break tradition. You should use 60 percent of your allotted fast break practice time for the fast-break individual skills. You could use more time at the learning stage if needed. You can cut back as the skills are overlearned.

Tips for Fast-Break Skill Instruction

You begin the preseason with the learning of fundamental individual skills of the fast break. You perfect these basic skills before going on to the more advanced moves. You do not want to put too much defensive pressure on the break during the learning period. You want to schedule inexperienced teams in your early predistrict games. Your players need the chance to become sold on your fast break attack to the point where they agree that any breakdown is their fault and not the fault of the system. Thus they will see the need to work harder, to concentrate better, to make the attack a winner.

You want to keep your practice moving at a fast tempo. Your practice sets the stage for the game tempo.

All your fast break drills should be executed at game tempo. But if you find a skill weakness, you can slow the tempo until that skill can be mastered. All your drills should be short. You can always come back to the drill later, or you can substitute a drill which teaches the same concepts but differs in its approach.

There is a drop in skill tone over the weekends. So don't be too harsh a critic on Mondays.

Whether you realize it or not your squad is constantly in competition with the other schools in your district every practice day. Each player should think and believe, when he leaves practice each night, that he has run harder, passed better, improved his balance, upgraded his rebounding, and played defense better than his competition. And more importantly, that he has challenged his own capabilities 100 percent.

Your fast break goal is to organize and control the ball movement at a tempo that is above the ability of the opposition to counter. The opponent's answers to limiting the success of your break involve defensive schemes geared to slow down your fast break tempo and offensive ideas which could amount to an all-out freeze. The fast break team must develop a strategy which will regain the up-tempo. Your fast break must continually pressure the defense. Your fast break may even pressure the opposition into running a counter fast break that is secondary to yours in their practice plans. No subordinate, practiced fast break attack will ever match your all-out organized and dedicated fast break.

Weaknesses of the Fast Break

Fast break errors can occur any place on the court and by any player. You will always have team teaching problems to solve. And there will always be player skills to learn before fast break success is assured. If you use extra practice time to bolster the learning of these skills, you will find that weaknesses can become strengths.

When the fast break advances the ball into the 16-foot area, your two offensive rebounders should get inside positioning as the shot is taken. If they do not, it is a grave error. It occurs mostly from the side shot areas with no pressure on the shot. The side shot looks inviting. You could run off several minutes trying to get that same good shot. You must put the responsibility on the rebounders to always achieve this preferred positioning. They should get in position quickly. Shooters should be aware of these rebounders going inside. It lessens the need for high percentage shots.

Another area of major weakness occurs when inexperienced players react mechanically in their break movements, in their filling of the lanes, in their habit passing. The players should understand that the break is a highly disciplined attack but it does allow some versatility. The break players should realize that, if they are to be successful in moving the ball to the basket, the greatest concentration and intensity are needed. But to run out of control is also an error. As coach you must determine proper speed for each particular player, for each unique team.

When players are not sure of the system, they will passively fill the passing lanes. This can be overcome by drilling the situations which may confront the fast break start and the fast break drive to the basket. A real problem exists when dribblers consistently take the ball all the way down one side of the floor.

Some other weaknesses you must control, change, or correct are: slowing the fast break tempo as it confronts defensive pressure; stopping the attack momentum as the break approaches the top of the key; failure to drive hard for the basket at every opportunity.

How the Fast Break Creates Board Pressures

The fast break attack concentrates on getting the ball down court ahead of the retreating opponents. This starts with the outlet pass. Opposition offensive patterns and strategy may try to take your best rebounders out of their position. You can counter this strategy in one of two ways: run a zone, keeping your rebounders in proper position; or run your man-to-man defense with constant lane assignments, regardless of where the offensive patterns take your primary rebounders.

You want to continue your fast break pressure even if your opponents are coming back in the early minutes of the game. This continued break pressure takes advantage of tired opponents. This is the time to try for a run of points. But be sure to watch your break carefully and slow it down if your team is tiring too fast.

The fast break adds another pressure when the opposition tenses as it tries to get back ahead of the ball. This extra tension causes opponents to try to match the break tempo. By playing above their regular tempo, they can make more and more mistakes, adding even more speed to your up-tempo.

You must practice anticipating fast break opportunities from every position on the floor. You must demand quick action, even though at times the players may read the play wrong. You want to keep the players aggressive, but you never want to let them make the same mistakes over and over.

You should study your players' moves, making sure all are moving into proper board position most of the time. This is true of the offensive boards as well as the defensive boards. A good fast break offense forces the opposition to pay more attention and devote more time to what the break will do. This limits their preparedness to keep you off of the offensive boards. Mentally, players may expect another pass before a shot in any passing pattern. This may catch opponents standing, or moving, in the wrong direction. It can happen to players on the perimeter, or players moving away from the basket. If the opposition begins to prepare just two or three days before the game, they cannot keep you off of the offensive boards. And just as the defensive boards is where your break begins, the offensive boards is where it ends.

How the Fast Break Develops Momentum Scoring Runs

You should not give your opponents an answering score without forcing them to pay a mental and physical price. The fast break scoring goal is consistency. To estimate your break efficiency, set up as a guide, 75 shots with 80 percent in the 60 percent shooting area.

A manager can keep a history of the number of times the break succeeded or failed. You should know who scored; what happened; which tactic or move allowed you to score; what option was used; whether it was from the primary break, the secondary phase, or the set offense. Diagram 1-1 displays a chart which will communicate this information to you. You record each possession, who scored and from where, and the option used to score. If the break failed, write why in the "which option" column. Diagram 1-1 will show if the break results from an opponent turnover (playing out of control or defensively forced) or from a hurried shot (rebound).

BREAKS	SCORE	WHICH OPTION WAS USED	HOW DID BREAK START?	COMMENT
1				
2				
3				
4				
5				
6				
7				
8				
9				
10				
11				
12				
13				
14				
15				
16				

Diagram 1-1

Players realize that by getting more nonpressure, close-in shots the fast break will produce a high shooting percentage. Your first team goal is to shoot within the 60- to 80-percent shooting areas.

It is difficult to measure the physical and emotional loss that comes from a fast break failure. Players should discipline themselves so that nothing less than 100 percent concentration and intensity will satisfy them. This insures success.

Fast break tempo also improves the game tempo in other parts of your game. A fast break tempo helps the player to realize his capabilities. It promotes a challenge for an all-out performance. But more importantly, fast break practices enable your team to shoot on balance at a higher tempo than your opponents. This frequently allows you to score while your opponents, playing at an unpracticed speed, miss.

A second fast break goal is to run several points on the scoreboard without your opponents scoring. These scoring runs are made by the strength of the break, or by the weakness of the opposition to answer. Scoring runs, with fast-break superior conditioning, can trigger hot shooting; or, on the other hand, it can cause an opponent's poor shooting. The more scoring runs the more your opponents may panic, become unglued, and actually try to speed up their tempo to catch up in a possession or two. This encourages even more scoring runs.

Scoring runs need some control to keep them at a tempo that can be maintained throughout the four quarters. In tough ball games you should use a controlled fast-break scoring spurt. You should put it on in the best time spots, according to the game movement. You do not allow your team to use it too long at any one time. You get the lead. This adds pressure to the opposition. To continually run, run, run leads to a race-horse, helter-skelter fast break system. It can force your own players into the style of play you wanted to impose on your opposition. But you still want to run at every opportunity. It is a delicate balance, orchestrated by you, the coach.

To run the break too long slows down the break attack. It encourages shooting from a lower shot percentage area, shooting pressure shots, and creating more floor errors as your players' concentration lags.

A scoring run means a cluster of baskets made by taking advantage of your opponents' mistakes or by increasing your game tempo. The opponent's failure to answer your scoring equals the start of the scoring run. This will develop an attitude and dedication to the fast-break scoring run style of play. A good running team actually feels uncomfortable trying to play at a slower tempo. The players feel the need for work to develop their skills to further the fast break success.

Your fast break team actually competes in every practice with your opponents. The practice winner usually wins on game night.

How the Fast Break Can Control Game Tempo

You should plan your practices so that the break's best pressure comes at specific times in the game. This increased tempo in practice sessions helps your team produce the same tempo in its games, even when the players are tired.

The fast break's best offensive efforts, or moves, should be practiced often. You must emphasize special game phases that can control the flow and ebb of the game. In your daily practice plan, you want to take time to scrimmage these specific game moves when your players are fresh—and also when they are tired.

The four most important time spans in a game are the first five minutes of each half and the last five minutes of each half.

1. In the first five minutes of the game you must set the game tempo and establish control.
2. In the last five minutes of the second quarter, you want to play your reserves. Their fresh condition should increase the tempo, and they should up-tempo the tired opposition.
3. In the first five minutes of the second half, your players must be fired up to stop the last gasp of your opponents as they try to take the tempo away from the fast break team.
4. In the last five minutes of the fourth quarter, when many games are won or lost, your players must know exactly what is expected of them.

Why the Fast Break Must Occupy Your Number-One Practice Position

You cannot get scoring results by just teaching the mechanical aspects of the break. Some coaches go to clinics and pick up diagrams on how to move the ball, how to execute the final drive for the shot—but they never seem to teach the break to perfection. When they are questioned later, they seem to be disillusioned about the results. The details in skill learning had been left out. This lack of knowledge causes turnovers and fewer shots at the basket. By teaching good execution of the break skills you will increase your shot opportunities and hold your turnovers to a minimum.

You cannot use the break and your set pattern offense with equal emphasis. The time element and your points of emphasis would hold both to a mediocre success. The team's mental attitude toward either one or the other would spell defeat. Although you need not commit yourself only to the fast break at the exclusion of a set offense, you must place the basic break foremost in your offensive scheme or it will never reach the level you desire.

How to Organize Your Fast Break Practice Sessions

The coach should take a few weeks out of the preseason time to draw up his season's master plan, then lay out his weekly goals. From this weekly plan he develops his daily plans. This early preparation will give him a big jump on the others who just gather up loose ends a week before the season begins.

Players respond to organized practices that move at a quick rate. Shorter drills usually are received better than longer ones. You can begin with a special talking period, but then get to work. Short-sentenced instruction and encouragement for a minute or two during time-out periods are helpful. You want to practice errors five or six times at these time-outs.

Let your mind photograph the good plays and the errors, and let them be the basis of your talk period. A famous football coach would watch a scrimmage practice for ten minutes, his mind photographing every play and every individual move, and he would call attention to the success or the mistakes that led to failures at the time-out periods. This coaching skill comes with experience. You can use a cassette recorder as an aid to recall, or you can make notes as needed. If you have enough substitutes, you could correct the error when a substitute goes on the floor. This method means practice never has to be stopped. But it also means you will not be generally discussing the error so all of the team can benefit.

Fast break and other offensive patterns are successful based on the skill level of each individual player. Choosing or fitting your offense to the capabilities of your squad is the big step toward a winning season. UCLA found out that you do not win games by saddling inexperienced players with several offenses. By dropping all patterns, except one simple high post pattern, they almost won a national championship with freshmen and sophomore players.

If you are fortunate enough to have four to six baskets in your gym, you can work out teaching stations for individual players to practice individual skill weaknesses. Five minutes should give a player time to execute a skill correctly 20 or 30 times. Teaching stations add more to good execution than five or six scrimmages.

Due credit can be given to an opponent's defense for forcing mistakes, but more mistakes come from your own team's lack of skills. You will see decided improvement in your fast break as you bear down on the individual instruction of ball handling, shooting, and rebounding skills.

Be sure to work hard to create the drill that will eliminate the error in the shortest time. You can set a skill drill at each station and let the players move every four or five minutes. The skill at each station can be changed from day to day according to the weaknesses that showed up in practice.

You want to keep the fast break tempo going at each station. The player should see and feel that the skill practice is related to increasing success in his scrimmage and game play. Keep the learning tempo equal to the game tempo. You can still slow it down if errors begin to crop up.

When errors do occur, your drill should emphasize control and balance, but you want to get back to your tempo rate as quickly as possible.

You want to challenge the total capabilities of your players to execute the fast break skills at game tempo at all times. A maximum controlled top speed is the goal you should strive for. One-count-stop and quick-shuffle-step plays are very important for accurate passing and ball control. To pass on time, at the instant the passing lane opens, and to eliminate the extra dribble that allows a lane to close, are basic to successful fast break penetration.

A single dribble should cover 6 to 10 feet in distance if you are to catch the defense out of position or outnumber them. You must eliminate the running pass off of one foot.

The fast break concept is an organized pattern for moving the ball down court by five players coordinated and under control at all times. The break must be flexible. Fast breaks make use of all the abilities of each player. But the 1-on-1 attack has its place in special situations. However, overuse of 1-on-1 maneuvers will call a halt to the motion of the other four players.

The fast break philosophy challenges the team's abilities at all times to capture the ball, move it, take opponents out of position, keep the passing lanes to the ball open, and be ready to drive for a lay-up or take the nonpressured, short jump shot at the instant it is open in the 60-percent shot area. And if the shot is missed, your rebounders capture the miss. This philosophy must be reflected in each practice session.

Players must be impressed and sold on the belief that passing and rebounding are the keys to the fast break's success. The drills must be arranged to teach quick tempo and discipline in passing, shooting, etc. You want your players to always pass with accuracy. That is the only way to keep control of the ball on the break. Your shooters will miss shots when forced to capture a ball passed in an awkward receiving position.

How to Make Use of Inexperienced Players

You may use your two best rebounders for only board responsibilities. If they are inexperienced, you would want to keep them out of the three-lane break. You could teach and develop their outlet passing abilities.

But if your best all-around athlete is inexperienced, you may designate him as the deep right guard rebounder. You want him to take the center lane cut. If he is a senior, you would want to train a sophomore so your program would not suffer. You always want to think about the future.

If your guards, 1 and 2, are inexperienced, you want them to receive the outlet pass, pass to the middle cutter, then fill the two outside lanes. Inexperienced guards are invariably dribblers. They must understand that the pass to the open man ahead of the ball is more important than the dribble.

Passing is the key to using inexperienced players successfully. You want to use short passes with inexperienced personnel, and you want to run the break with your two or three best ball movers. You have to get a good shot as quickly as possible. This cuts down on turnovers.

If one guard is shaky, you would use him to screen a release for the pass and then pass back to the playmaker at the end of the secondary phase of the break. You would also want him to run the fly pattern of the break. If the high post can control the ball, you could let the playmaker pass to him before getting the ball back. You would want to limit the use of the shaky guard.

If you have inexperienced post players, you allow your best ball handling guard to move occasionally into high post play. You would want to be careful about your big, inexperienced players putting the ball into a dribble situation, especially from the high post key area to the low post. Work on their pivots, big steps, and carrying the ball through pressure with both hands (as in the blast-out rebounding technique).

You must not let the inexperienced players forget that the purpose of running the break is to get the nonpressured shot inside the 16-foot area. Inexperienced players may work as the long sideline cutter, player 1, regardless of whether they are a guard, forward, or center. Your fast break pattern may use the side lane to execute a variation if you are just too inexperienced.

You should attack from the weak side a few times to keep the defense aware of the first penetration attack. But whatever you do, you want to limit the number of options for inexperienced players. If your squad lacks a good rebounder, you want to emphasize blocking out the opponents and holding the advantage. You may use a switching man-to-man defense which will always give proper starting block-out positioning.

The Picture-Perfect Basic Break

Before going any further we will present the bare-bone basic break. Then as the book develops we will adjust it, show variations to it, and share all the possible options of both the basic break and its variations.

Diagram 1-2 illustrates the basic fast break motion stripped to its first mechanical movements. The center lane cutter is the most important ball mover in the break. But all positions on the break are important if the ball is to be moved swiftly and successfully. The outlet pass quickness of the rebounder and the initial receiver's quick pass into the hands of the center lane cutter will determine the success of the break. The goal of every fast break move is to have controlled speed with enough quickness to maintain at least a one-player advantage over the defense.

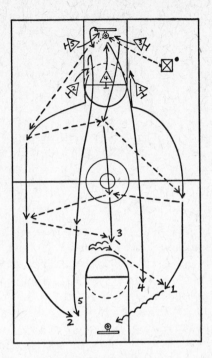

Diagram 1-2

The point player, who runs the center lane cut, moves the ball to the head of the key. His passing and motion will dictate who gets the lay-up drive. He passes to a nonpressured shot position; or he dribble-drives forcing a defender to stop him. Then he passes to the open wing. This pass to one of the wings should find rebounders 4 and 5 moving to the offensive board rebound positions.

Simple, isn't it? And different from the popular number break. What makes it so effective is its versatility. Options, developed from years of seeing all kinds of defensive roadblocks, renders it unstoppable. At every instance each attacker has more options than there are possible defenders. The primary break suddenly evolves into a secondary break. And then, without stopping to reset, the break is into your half-court set offense. All of these maneuvers are fully explained and illustrated. Drills are presented which will show you how to train your team as well as emphasize individual skills. And should your personnel be less than perfect for the fast break, alternate courses will be offered.

Diagram 1-3 pictures the position of the team when it is ready to go up for the rebound and release for the fast break. Players get to these positions in a variety of ways. The easiest method of securing them is to begin in a zone. However, these zone rebound positions can be reached from man-to-man by releasing at the shot and flashing to them. This, of course, is weaker than just boxing out and letting different players as-

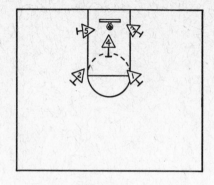

Diagram 1-3

sume different fast-break lane filling roles. This latter method requires a little more fast break teaching. But players should have some experience at each position and be able to handle the position fairly well.

Players 3 and 4 may, for example, interchange positions depending upon how similar their skills are. Most coaches will place player 3 at the rebound triangle right wing, because they feel that 3 would be able to get out on the break sooner. Player 3, taking the rebound, would pass to the outlet receiver and take the center lane. Players 4 and 5, your top rebounders, go hard to the defensive boards. If either one gets the rebound, he passes to outlet receiver 1 or 2. Players 1 and 2 are long rebounders and outlet pass receivers. Player 5 is in a better position for a right-handed outlet pass throw and to get out-of-bounds fast should the opposition score.

Player 3 should be the best basketball player, the top athlete on your squad. He blocks out, reads the rebound, and cuts down the center lane. He should take the center lane on the fast break at every opportunity. The only time a pass should not be directed to player 3 in the center lane is when a defensive player is stationed there. Player 3, under that condition, should clear the area for player 4 to receive the pass into the middle lane. Player 4 then can reverse the ball while player 3 races on a fly pattern.

SECRETS OF DEVELOPING
THE INDIVIDUAL FOR
FAST BREAK BASKETBALL

2

Coaches of fast break teams must do a good selling job on the idea that players in top playing condition have the most fun, as they find that their skills are successful—especially in the all-important fourth quarter. Great satisfaction is found by playing at a level that challenges all of their capabilities. Conditioning is the basis for clutch playing and skill level staying power.

Good condition guarantees you the greatest freedom to play the game. Gaining this level of play does not come easily. The players must be willing to pay the price. There are two levels of fast break conditioning: the physical and the mental. Running programs enable your athletes to achieve physical conditioning. But mental conditioning depends on the attitude, philosophy, and psychology of the coach.

This mental and physical effort is one base for a multiple run of points. There are times when opponents of the fast break lose the timing of their patterns while trying to slow and control the fast break tempo. Winning the battle calls for condition superiority, less turnovers, best percentage shooting, rebounding, and superior passing. The fast break team that works on deep-running practice sessions will have a playing advantage over the opposition.

Top conditioning creates the stamina for maximum sustained efforts on both boards throughout all four quarters. It increases the control and confidence in fourth quarter shooting, and it provides the ability to play both offense and defense at a greater tempo than the opposition.

First-rate fast breaking teams develop good anticipation for fast breaking from any place on the floor and from any situation. Fast breaking from turnovers, steals, off the defensive boards, and after made shots, must be practiced and developed. Here is where mental conditioning pays dividends. It is a matter of outnumbering defenders who are ahead of the ball. The key to taking advantage of every opportunity to fast break is the constant upcourt look by every player. Look ahead of any dribble, or at the instant of gaining possession of the ball. Thinking break on every ball touched or captured when the fast break team is playing defense should trigger a lane-filling break. The fast break team is always conscious of having the ball slapped into an open space or intercepted when playing defense. The players nearest the fast-break running lanes fill the lanes, always shouting: "I've got the side (or center) lane."

How to Develop the Positive Running Approach

If you have not tried a total running program, try this. In early fall set up an easy Fartlek Cross Country program which gradually shifts to two days a week of multiple sprints. During the last two or three weeks before going on the floor, have the sprinters do field line running. You want to cover about half the football field; or for variety run the bleacher steps, or you could use a large circle. You could have the team follow the leader and run for variation. While using the circle run, your players could be taught a change of pace, weaving maneuvers, front reverses, jump-left balance, jump-right balance, pivoting, backward running, shuffle right, and shuffle left. You should try to use every maneuver possible which emphasizes balance.

But don't use running as a penalty for errors committed in practice. You can accomplish more positive results by giving your players multiple tries at executing the skill correctly. You must stop the scrimmage and comment on the error, even correct it. You could maybe practice the correction four or five times. You could develop a drill which will correct the error; or you could use the ones presented in this book. It should take about two or three minutes, but it helps the player execute correctly under pressure.

You want your full-court drills run with correct passes, dribbles which emphasize ball protection moves, dribbling which permits peripheral vision to pass to a teammate as he releases from his opponent, and downcourt vision which requires a pass to a teammate ahead of the ball. You can combine these into one running drill, or you can use a drill which teaches each skill separately. You can begin the year with separate drills and work toward the drills which combine skills.

Your running program should develop your fast break tempo. It should increase physical and mental endurance. The mental endurance starts to set the pace long before the player reaches his complete physical tiredness.

Be sure to have a good physical examination of each player before the running program and season starts. Also have one more examination after four or five weeks of work. Set up a weekly weight chart, using the early examination weight as a guide. Several checks during the season will reveal who stays in shape, who is growing stale, and who may need a different type of conditioning.

You are striving to build the confidence of each player in his ability to run with more controlled abandonment. This effort not only emphasizes safety, but encourages enjoyment, anticipation, and concentration in each player.

After your outside running program ends and you move inside, you do not want to waste the conditioning achieved. You immediately begin an inside running program. This inside program should teach the fundamentals of fast break basketball as well as maintain the developed conditioning.

Fundamentals are essential to fast break basketball. More time must be spent rebounding and passing (outlet passing, passing from the receiver to the middle lane, and the three-lane thrust to the basket for the score) than in any other offensive attack. If you are not willing to devote such time to fundamentals, then fast break basketball will never be successful for you.

In its simplest form fast break basketball consists of three parts: rebounding, outlet passing, and lane filling. Other items then come from your philosophy: shot selection, secondary break, etc. Several drills are offered here to enable you to condition and develop these fundamentals.

2-on-1 drill

Procedure (Diagram 2-1):

1. Line up two lines of offensive players and one defender.
2. You can require passing (as shown in Diagram 2-1), or you can allow dribbling to escape X1 should X1 decide to come high on the floor to defend.
3. Whoever scores becomes the next X1. If X1 steals a pass, the passer becomes the new X1. If X1 rebounds an errant shot, the shooter becomes the new X1.
4. The other two players sprint to the two lines at the other end of the floor. This sprint is important for conditioning.
5. You could require a baseball pass or a two-handed overhead outlet pass by X1 to either line 1 or line 2.
6. You could run the drill as two wings (as in Diagram 2-1) or you could run with a middle man and a wing.

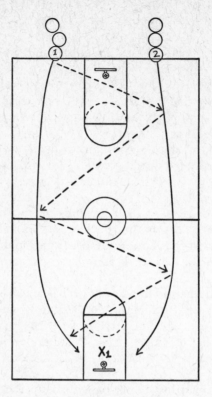

Diagram 2-1

Objectives:

1. To teach 1 and 2 to attack 2-on-1.
2. To teach X1 to defend against a 2-on-1 situation.

3-on-1 drill

Procedure (Diagram 2-2):

1. Line up three lines of offensive attackers and one defender.
2. You want three lines to arrive at different times. Then you can stagger the lines or require one to sprint ahead of another.
3. Whoever throws the ball away or shoots becomes the next X1.
4. The other three sprint to other end of the floor and the end of the three offensive lines.
5. You could require X1 to throw an outlet pass or baseball pass to line 3. Meanwhile 1 and 2 have begun their fly patterns. This would get your attack into staggered lines.

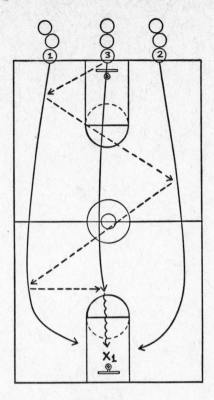

Diagram 2-2

Objectives:

1. To teach 3, 2, and 1 to attack a lone defender on a 3-on-1 fast break.
2. To teach X1 to defend against a three-man attack.

3-on-2 drill

You use the same procedures and objectives, just add an X2 as another defender. You can require the two defenders to play tandem or parallel or give them freedom of choice. Whoever shoots or throws the ball away sprints to the opposite three offensive lines with X1 and X2. The other two offensive players stay as the new X1 and X2.

3-on-2-on-1 drill

Procedure (Diagram 2-3):

1. Line up three offensive players and two defenders.

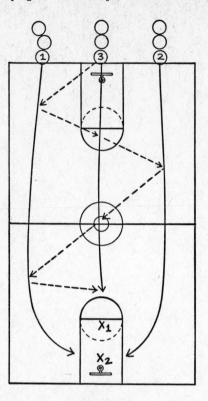

Diagram 2-3

2. You attack as in the 3-on-2 drill.

3. Whoever scores or throws the ball away becomes the lone defender as **X1** and **X2** attack 2-on-1 on the way back downcourt.

4. The other two original attackers stay as the new **X1** and **X2**.

Objectives:

1. To teach a 3-on-2 passing attack.
2. To teach a 2-on-1 attack.
3. To teach defense of a 3-on-2 attack.
4. To teach defense of a 2-on-1 attack.

3-on-3-on-3-on-3 drill

Procedure (Diagram 2-4):

1. If you have a 12-man squad lineup as in Diagram 2-4, make it a 4-on-4-on-4. If you have a 16-man squad, make it a 4-on-4-on-4-on-4.

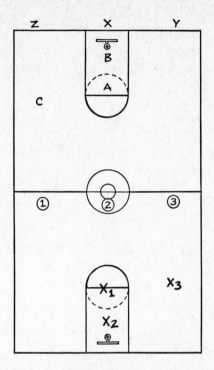

Diagram 2-4

2. 1, 2, and 3 attack X1 and X2 as in the 3-on-2 drill. X3 cannot defend.

3. When X1 or X2 rebounds the outlet pass to X3, X1 and X2 read X3's move and fill the lanes for a fast break.

4. X1, X2, and X3 then fast break against A, B, and C. 1, 2, and 3 stay on defense. If 1, 2, or 3 scored, X2 would inbounds the ball to X3 and they would run a fast break after a score.

5. When A and B stop X1, X2, and X3, they outlet pass to C and fast break against 1, 2, and 3. Only two of 1, 2, and 3 would be on defense.

6. X, Y, and Z step on the floor and get ready for 1, 2, and 3's fast break attack. X1, X2, and X3 step off of the floor.

7. The drill continues in this manner for an allotted time period or it can be scored by designating a number of baskets to be scored.

8. You can, after learning to attack full court presses, allow the attackers-turned-defenders to press after their scores. This can be a man-to-man press or a zone press.

Objectives:

1. To learn to play continuously in a 3-on-2 fast break setting.
2. To condition.

3. To learn to score, then jump into a press.

4. To learn to attack a press with the same pattern as the fast break.

5. To learn to fast break after a score.

The Fast Break's First Fundamental: One-Count-Stop-and-Shuffle Step

A player moving at a controlled speed should be capable of a one-count-stop which enables him to front-pivot, or reverse, with either foot. He should be able to pass, or shoot, or drive according to the situation.

The shuffle step is a skip made at controlled speed, without losing momentum. The skip should come just before the ball hits the receiver's hands. Both feet are off the floor as the ball hits the receiver's hands. This skill gives the player better balance for passing and shooting, and it provides an opportunity to change directions or continue with the dribble drive.

Your Fast Break Goals

Versatile teams do not run behind the defensive roadblocks. They cut over the defender to get a ballside position to receive the pass. This move eliminates the lob pass; but it gets the driving lay-up and possible 3-point play with a minimum chance of a turnover.

There are five primary team goals which must be accomplished, practiced, and perfected if the break is to achieve optimum success. Your goals:

1. To have your rebounder capture the ball and pass successfully to the outlet player.

2. To have passes thrown with accuracy and not be telegraphed.

3. To get the lanes filled quickly and on time.

4. To vary the running lanes so you can eliminate the defensive roadblocks.

5. To keep the passing lanes open as you streak down the court.

How to Develop Balance—The Fast-Break Skill Foundation

Balance is vital to the successful execution of the fast break skills. Some players seem to be blessed with a natural ability to execute skills rapidly. Others must develop better balance before adding to their skills. But you can help speed up balance which in turn enables them to gain more efficient skills. Your time allocated to improving a player's balance is time well spent.

Good balance increases the tempo of offensive and defensive play. The weakest player on the starting team generally sets the tempo. In past years, coaches had a tendency to write off the awkward player. They spent more time with the smaller, quicker players. Today however coaches start to work early with the tall players. Parked under the basket, they are given all kinds of ball handling and shooting drills.

Balance improvement can come through physical maturation, weight lifting, exercises, and skill drills. Lack of balance can be seen in these areas: changing directions, lateral shuffle change, slowing down in order to execute stops, unbalanced rebounds, poor pivot control, out-of-control moving or dribbling, slowness in jumping.

Some exercises which will improve balance

1. Start in a flex position, jumping 3 to 5 feet left and right, catching your balance, and landing on one foot each time.
2. Speed jumping the squares—the small square comes first, then the larger ones, to maintain your speed.
3. Multiple broad jumps.
4. Running backwards.
5. Standing and multiple hopping on left then right foot.
6. Lateral shuffle with opponent attempting to throw you off-balance.

Drills which will improve balance and basketball skill execution

1. Weave running—direction changes.
2. Jump stops.
3. Rebounding—wrist snap chest passes.
4. Dribble stops and pivots
5. Fake and dribble
6. Moving jump pass to a moving target.

Physical strength development will add a great deal to balance Strength and rapid growth seldom go hand in hand with taller players. Weight lifting at least three days a week, 15 to 20 minutes, can speed up the development of body strength. The program should include strength lifts, speed lifts, and fast instep lifts. Emphasize strength work, and balance, for the legs, shoulders, arms and hands. These are the major areas for fast breaking players.

Coaches can either wait on natural body maturity, or they can speed up body balance. Because body balance is very essential to the fast break game, the above drills can help you speed up balance.

How to Develop Individual Fast-Break Rebounding Skills

The rebounding skill and outlet pass that starts the fast break puts a premium on the player's height, ability to jump, aggressiveness, timing, reading the rebound, and outlet passing ability. You cannot overlook quickness, blocking out, positioning, and the quick jump-up to retrieve the ball that can counter players who are taller and slower. So don't sell your team short in rebounding until hours have been spent perfecting the details of quick rebounding. UCLA parlayed quick rebounders into a team that beat several teams of superior height, strength, and weight.

In preparing for your rebound drills, be sure that your players are physically and mentally prepared for the rebound contact. Muscle stretching, muscle strength, and multiple jumps become absolutely necessary. To help eliminate the sprained ankles that may cause one or more players to lose several days of practice, you should provide ankle wraps or tape the ankles.

Your earlier drills should cover the one-step rebound, reading shots from the different angles, reading the arc of the shot, then considering the distance. All of these qualities demand player adjustments. Check the player's reading, timing, and aggressive control. You also want your rebounder to look out on the court as he comes down with the carom. After the single rebounder drill, you work the rebounders in pairs. Rebounders should block out, then go to the board aggressively. While drilling in pairs, make sure the rebounders pick the shot up at the apex of the arc and read the ball on its way down to the basket. The rebounders must race to the position where the ball will ricochet. It does a rebounder no good to have inside position but be on the side of the basket away from the carom. It also does the rebounder no good to be where the ball comes off the board but be behind an opponent.

Timing is also a key ingredient of successful rebounding. In rebounding at the high school or college level, 90 percent of the balls taken off the board are below the rim of the basket. Yet eight out of ten high school players can jump and touch the rim. Why then are most rebounds taken off of the board nearly 2 feet below the rim? Standing, poor timing, rebounding attitude, and a lack of intensity are the culprits. Your team rebounding skills will be great if you place rebounding ahead of defense and offense.

The blockout is the rebounding equalizer

The blockout, or checking your opponent before rebounding, is the best equalizing skill for controlling the boards against superior height. Successful rebounders work daily on jumping and conditioning. Tiredness is an enemy of consistent board play over four quarters. Drilling for board condition should be added to fast break and defensive conditioning.

Rebounding positioning and clearing the board can be taught efficiently by using game condition drills. The earlier drills must emphasize the individual skills, followed by concentrating on three-player triangle positioning. You want to work first on three- to six-step positioning in front of the basket. Then you want to throw various types of ball arcs for the rebounders to read, especially the flat shot which produces the quick bounce that often clears the jumper's hands.

You want to analyze your rebounder's action and reaction. You point out the successes and give him a chance to correct any particular error. You strive for confidence and relaxation, eliminate tension and fear. The first hard physical contacts may cause a loss of intensity. Some players are naturally aggressive, others will use a "feel your way" approach. The latter group needs more maturity to be good rebounders. Daily you want to coordinate and emphasize practicing the blockout, reading the shot, and going to the ball. As practice continues, you add the passout with accuracy to complete the rebound skill. Running the fast break does not give you playing stamina for the multiple jumps required for rebounding during an entire game. Only by drilling multiple jumps will your players become quick and continuous rebounders.

All players should develop the habit of calling "shot" as an opponent starts lifting the ball. This helps to teach your players to look for early keys which signal when an opponent is about to shoot. The blockout should be set in motion before the offensive rebounder can react. This forces the opponent to hesitate, or to change direction, thus throwing off the opposition's rebound timing.

After the blockout, rebounders should return hard to the board with quick steps, body flexed, ready to go up on any step to snare the ball. Don't let your players hold the block so long that they take themselves out of the rebound action. Utilize short shot rebounds under the basket. This means a quick-step boxout, then a quicker return for the rebound. Outside shots provide more time to react; you may hold longer on the blockout. Proper timing, well-drilled, gives your players extra momentum to jump for the rebound.

Vision on the ball should be picked up at the shot's downward flight in order to get a quick read as it hits the basket. Rebounders get off the floor as the ball hits the basket or the board. Some rebounders wait to have the ball come to the rebounder. But great rebounders go after the ball.

The details of drilling rebounds are an important part in developing efficient habits that stay with the rebounder throughout the game against the toughest pressure. The drills should cover standing multiple jumps; one-, two-, three-, or four-step jumps; stutter steps to the board to rebound; tipping on the board and recovering; tip pass to spots with the rebound (corner area for this fast break); and rebounding with one or two players standing under the basket, to force the rebounder to see the ball and the players at the same time while rebounding.

The drills should be illustrated and explained carefully. Be sure to add quick-up rebounding drills to the daily program. You can change the order frequently during the season. Emphasis on rebounding will add to the fast break because most breaks begin off of the boards.

Do not lose patience if failures arise, as they will. Be able to call a halt and come back to the drill later. The "do or else" approach will soon destroy the player's enthusiasm to master this important drill and skill; several short drills with a good tempo seem better than the long drills. Be sure to change the position of shots up on the board and the position of the rebounders. This will make the drill a real game condition experience.

Rebounding strengths and errors

Many rebounders start from a standing position which forces them to flex down before going up for the rebound. Rebounders should begin with their knees bent. They should play their entire game from this bent position. In fact, moving in a flexed position is like having your rifle cocked ready to fire. Rebounders should leave the floor with an extra thrust-off of their inside foot. This allows a player to go up and out. This up-and-out movement gives rebounders clearance for the outlet pass.

Details of the final steps for capturing and controlling the ball are important in order to keep the ball protected. Rebounders must go up hard, with arms fully extended, hands fairly close together, wrist cocked, and fingers cupped in a normal spread. The fingers, as they capture the ball, should be placed firmly past the center of the ball. They then bring their hands forward and twist, putting the throwing hand back of the ball. This move also helps to twist off other hands that may be on the ball. On the way down rebounders should work to achieve an outlet passing position.

Good rebounders protect the ball with their elbows and move their arms on the way down. They don't pull the ball down to their laps. A fast, smaller player will get it or slow the outlet pass. Bringing the ball up to outlet pass is telegraphing your move. If the rebounder is pressured from both sides on the way down from the rebound, teach him to take the rebound all the way to the floor, reverse-pivot, and dribble out to make the pass. This is called the blastout technique. Player 3 must be particularly adept at executing the blastout. Other players may need only one dribble on their blastout techniques; but player 3 should be able to handle the ball all the way down court if necessary.

Guides to reading rebounds

During the early instruction period while the learner is attempting to read the rebound direction, you can suggest several aids for capturing the rebound, especially its distance and direction.

1. Expect flat shots to come off of the board or the iron fast.
2. The length of your rebound position away from the board depends on the length of the outside shot.
3. Most angled outside shots will bound away from the front of the basket if missed.
4. Corner shots, if pressured and hurried, will be missed by overshooting, which makes the weakside rebound position very important.
5. Nonpressured corner shots will generally fall short when missed.
6. High-arced shots, dropping almost straight down at the basket, will bounce up, or hang, which makes this shot the easiest to rebound.
7. You can learn a great deal by rebounding your own shots.

The crucial key to the fast break is the timing and quickness needed to capture the rebound and execute a successful pass to the outlet receiver. The triangle rebounders realize that their execution must beat the opponents' ability to get back in front of the ball. You do not have a primary fast break unless the break players outnumber their opponents.

A key to a successful fast break is the depth of the outlet pass. The outlet pass should be out near the ten-second line. The passer and the outlet receiver must have an eye contact and make a fine judgment regarding the length of the pass determined by the defensive pressure.

Offensive and defensive rebounding drills

Diagrams 2-5, 2-6, and 2-7 illustrate drills for single- and multiple-players' aids in rebound instruction. They should be repeated regularly for rebound positioning, and timing must be practiced until it is a habit. Don't give up on the importance of rebounding or lose patience.

The single drills illustrate 1-on-1 rebounding used in several floor positions (Diagram 2-5). You want to start close to the basket and move up the floor about two steps at a time. Diagram 2-5 shows offensive player O faking down toward the low post areas, then, with a quick reverse, flashing up to the free-throw line to receive a pass and shoot. Rebounder X moves up to pressure the shot and for a possible right-hand dribble. His hand and body should go up vertically to eliminate fouling. Pressure the right side and arm of the right-handed shooter.

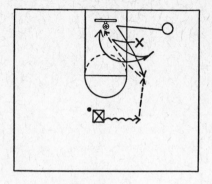

Diagram 2-5

Obscure the shooter's vision with the hand when you cannot reach the shot hand. Remember your hand pressure is trying to force the shooter to change his shot arc. Don't drop your hand.

Use vertical vision to see an opponent's initial move toward the basket and the flight of the ball. As you hit the floor, reverse-pivot in the direction of the shooter's first move toward the basket. Right-handed shooters generally shoot right. You can add the outlet pass to X's aggressive rebound. This not only teaches defensive rebounding, but it allows you to develop individual defense, individual offense, and offensive movement without the ball. You can require the offensive player to pass back to the original passer should his 1-on-1 fake not free him for a shot. You could also require the defender to take the ball out-of-bounds on made shots. This would simulate getting the fast break going after a made basket or free throw.

Diagram 2-6 depicts various off-of-the-shot positions taken by player O. If you are familiar with the opponent's offensive patterns, you can use the shot positions where most of their shooting would take place.

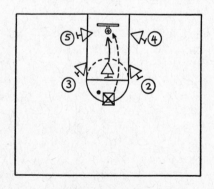

Diagram 2-6

Your drills should be short for increased shot pressure, blockout, and successful rebounding. The shooter should fake before shooting, forcing defenders to read the start of the shot. The shooter, manager or coach, can dribble around the court; shoot high arc one time, low arc the next; from a great distance one time, from close in the next—to impel defenders to read the shot and get to their proper rebounding positions.

This drill can also incorporate offensive rebounding. The O's should use the offensive steps and techniques which you intend to teach.

Again, if the rebounder secures the boards, he should outlet-pass; and the team can fast break to the other end of the court. If the basket is made, the designated player to throw the ball in can begin the fast break after a made basket.

An unpardonable sin of rebounding is for a rebounder to stand behind his opponent's rebound position. He either fouls or watches the rebound from the rear. Drill your rebounders to move to any slot that is not occupied: at least require an even positioning. When the fast break rebounder occupies a secondary position, he must go for a percentage rebound position. He knows where the ball will ricochet (see Guides to reading rebounds), so his movement should be to that position on the floor. If your player gets inside position, he has a better chance to capture the rebound.

Diagram 2-7 illustrates a basic 2-on-2 moving drill. You may start the 2-on-2 from a still position but move quickly to game speed for a real game-like experience. This drill can help teach the mechanics of your man-to-man defense. It can compel your defenders to be ever alert to two hands coming together on the ball, the first indication that a shot is forthcoming. This drill can also emphasize offensive rebounding. You can require an outlet pass after a defensive rebound by stationing a player near midcourt.

Diagram 2-8 illustrates a three-player weave. But you should use parts of your next opponent's offense. Players are actually playing

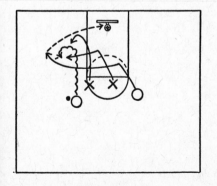

Diagram 2-7   **Diagram 2-8**

3-on-3 in the game-like drill, especially when you are using your next opponent's offense. Upon securing the rebound, an outlet pass is thrown and the break is underway. On a score, you could designate a player to throw the ball in and begin your break after a made shot.

This drill not only simulates actual game competition, but it is also highly competitive. And when run at the full-court level, it is a game conditioner.

Diagram 2-9 is an offensive rebounding drill for fast break shots that are missed. It illustrates positioning one or two defenders under the basket. This will teach your offensive rebounder that it is possible to watch the ball and to see open slots for rebounding while playing at full speed. This drill emphasizes going to the board without going over the backs of defensive rebounders. The drill also cuts down the number of times that a rebounder stops behind an opponent's rebound position. The drill impresses upon the rebounder the necessity to continue attacking the boards, even if caught behind a defender in the percentage rebound position. If you are moving, trying to secure an even position, rebounds will come your way, even when caught in a secondary rebounding position.

This also illustrates the development of vertical vision, seeing the apex of the shot-arc and the shooter at the same time. Although blocked

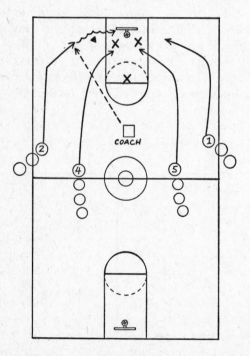

Diagram 2-9

out hard, the rebounders read the ball while going toward the primary rebounding areas, even if one or two under-the-basket defenders are already stationed there. Your rebounding players should see the ball in flight and be aware of the open rebound slots. They go to the basket hard without fouling. Your fast break thrust does not end until you fail to recover the offensive rebound. Then you go back on defense and get ready to fast break again.

The drill begins with players 4 and 5 at midcourt. Players 4 and 5 begin running toward the basket, simulating a fast break trailer (Diagram 2-9). When player 4 or 5 reaches the key area, the coach (or manager) passes to 1 or 2 who shoots immediately. This simulates a shot being taken from the wings on the fast break. Players 4, 5, and the nonshooting wing (player 1 or 2) go to the offensive boards. Two of the three have the primary rebounding areas covered; and the other one is protecting the secondary rebounding area. If the break fails to score, you should get a second shot.

Secrets of Individual Fast-Break Passing Fundamentals

Simple fast break drills, with emphasis on specific skills, insure a winning season. Two of the most important skills for fast break success are rebounding and passing. Rebounding has been fully covered. We now move to passing.

Do not teach too many pass options at one time. Learning new skills and developing them daily throughout the season provides the best results for your coaching efforts.

At the start of fall practice, the most experienced players should work the hardest to tone their passing skills. A bad passing habit can be picked up at any time during the season. Passing details need the same emphasis as rebounding details if you are to attain your fast break goals. Total concentration always pays the greatest dividends. The most experienced player should set the top practice tempo. He should never let it die down. Upperclassmen should always be ready to help the new players.

The most important ingredient for pattern success is accurate passing. Along with accuracy you must emphasize that the pass be delivered on time—not too early, not too late. There is that moment when the receiver is open, when he is ahead of the defense, when he has worked to clear himself. At that precise instant, the pass must be delivered accurately.

At times, some coaches become intrigued with teaching certain patterns they think will be the answers to counter various defenses. But a struggling offense may bring these coaches around to the realization that most of the offense depends on the passing skill of the least experienced player.

If you have a green team, you must take the time to discipline their passing. By passing well, without many turnovers, your team can win against teams that have more experience in other phases of the game.

Diagram 2-10 exhibits a simple parallel line passing drill. By having a simple, easy-to-learn drill, the performers can put all their concentration into learning skill details. In this drill, a middle-weaving player, or coach, walks the curved line to make targets for the bounce pass drill. Pass receivers must step to meet the pass, a most important habit to form.

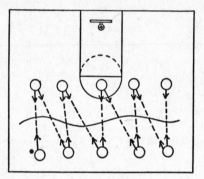

Diagram 2-10

You may add more game conditioning experience by setting the lines farther apart. You can require both lines to move or change sides. This forces the passer to practice bounce passing to a moving target.

You start practicing on the details of the chest pass and the shoulder baseball pass. You begin by using the same drill positions as shown in Diagram 2-10. You advance to the movement of Diagram 2-11. Everyone can throw the ball at a general target, but few can really pass with accuracy to a moving target. By limiting movement in the early learning stages, you can impel more concentrated effort on the actual skill development.

Diagram 2-11 displays the two-line, moving target drill. This drill provides multiple uses, such as moving to receive the hand-off pass using single, two, or three dribbles followed by a pass, and players changing sides. You can use the same drill format to develop the side arm pass, the chest pass, the shoulder baseball pass, and the overhead outlet pass. You can add practice execution of the jab step and pivot, use of the head-and-shoulder fake before passing, a change of pace before passing, the shuffle dribble, and the front cross dribble.

Proper upcourt vision of the moving teammate by the dribbler before passing must be emphasized in fast break basketball. Number each player, then you let them pass according to the number. You want finally to expand the drill over the half-court.

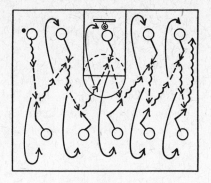

Diagram 2-11

You want to hold dribbling-passing drills to only one, two, or three dribbles before passing. Don't allow a dribbler to go on an ego trip. The greedy dribbler will kill your team patterns. If he does not have passing skills, he will dribble your team into trouble. A good dribbler should be like a sixth player on the court, forcing the defense out of ballside position and hitting the open player. Poor use of the dribble can limit the effectiveness of your other four players.

If you can develop one pass which is quick and accurate, you can develop others. Learning how to execute three or four passes, and using good judgment to choose the right pass for the specific situation, increases the playmaking ability of the passer and enhances the ability of the fast break team to zip up and down the floor. Passing also furthers the fast break's ability to penetrate the defense. The player who develops passing abilities adds more flexibility to his game, and he can force the roadblocks to react after the pass is made. It takes more work and discipline, not only to execute the passes, but also to make the correct judgment in choosing the right pass.

Fast-break passing points of emphasis

The right pass increases the number of opportunities the fast break can take advantage of to penetrate various defensive roadblocks. Passing is the major attack weapon which moves the ball through the defense to the high-percentage shot areas. Players should set high goals for pass efficiency such as no interceptions and less than three passes touched per player per game. Each year, regardless of experience, your drills should start with a detailed review of a specific pass skill.

Your drilling should follow a progressive outline: for example, you begin teaching the chest pass to a stationary player, who steps to receive; then you go on to passing to a moving player. While doing these elementary drills, players concentrate on the details of a quick release. They throw strikes to hand targets with a quick, short follow-through. You change passing distances in order to learn the right speed for various pass lengths.

For some reason, many players, who receive passes on the run, hold their arms down close to their bodies. They must be drilled to carry their arms above their hips, and to reach out to receive the pass with the elbows slightly flexed. They should cushion the ball in, then quickly snap the pass to a teammate. That is fast break passing.

Running with the arms high is a good game conditioner. Tired arms will drop.

Passing and receiving will shortly, when drilled correctly, become a single skill. Your drills should place the same emphasis on receiving the ball as they do on passing it.

If you allow careless execution in passing the ball, such carelessness will haunt you all season. And the more carelessness you allow during practice the more the players will be careless during a game. Players must overcome throwing the pass at a teammate in a general receiving area. On-the-button passes are absolutely essential for the fast moving receiver to catch and pass, in a fluid motion, as he moves at a fast break tempo.

Poor passes can force the receiver to miss shots. Poorly thrown or poorly received passes require time to adjust before passing again. Poorly thrown or received passes allow the defense time to react back on what once was a wide open receiver. One bad pass seems to set off a series of bad passes, as each passer tries to recover from the first bad pass.

Where most turnovers occur in fast break basketball

By eliminating turnovers you can get more shots at the basket. And fast break teams usually commit more turnovers than teams who play at a slower tempo. Knowledge of where most turnovers occur will help to reduce those turnovers:

1. The quick fake-and-dribble. The ball must have the dribble hand on top before the pivot foot moves. Too much traveling occurs in fake-and-drive situations and in pivots as the players pass and run at full speed.
2. Capturing a free ball on the floor. The ball must stay in virtually the same position as it was at the time of capture. Any rolling, sliding, or moving as you try to pass is generally called traveling.
3. When on the move, catching the ball with one foot on the floor then taking a one-two step results in a call for traveling.

4. Meeting defensive pressure as you pivot causes the pivot foot to shift. If the player always exercises downcourt vision, much of this will be eliminated.

5. Taking a pass then stepping too far impels the receiver to drag the pivot foot.

6. While running at a fast break speed, the receiver catches the pass and continues on a step or two. This happens a lot at the end of the break when a lay-up follows the walk.

7. Receiving an outlet pass without seeing down court. The outlet pass receiver has his back to the downcourt lanes. He receives a pass and turns to dribble all in one motion. A defensive man is standing there and the receiver walks.

8. When leaving the floor to pass, the player's motion carries him forward into a defender impelling the charging call. This happens when the center lane dribbler goes beyond the foul line after passing to a teammate for a lay-up.

9. Taking too many steps after receiving a pass from the middle lane man before you lay the ball in the basket.

10. Carrying the ball by beginning with the hand under the ball from a pivot start.

11. Intercepting a pass and immediately pushing the ball into the dribble with one or both hands.

12. Leaving the floor to pass, or shoot, and having the ball blocked into the player's hands as he lands on the floor.

13. Allowing the dribble to get too high, which forces the player to cock his wrist and carry the ball.

14. Dribbler drives into a switch surprise, forcing a foot travel.

15. Out of control or running the lanes, looking directly at a passer instead of using peripheral vision. This type of lane running usually results in an off-of-the-ball charging call.

16. Coming down with the rebound and passing it without proper downcourt vision.

17. Out of control, with opponent stepping into player's lane while running; or out of control, with opponent stepping into an intended passing lane.

18. Charging into a defender under the basket as you try to score on a lay-up.

19. Not taking the ball low enough when you try a blastout technique.

Secrets of the fast break bounce pass fundamentals

You can set up a bounce pass drill for several specific uses: a quick bounce to the inside post men, a quick bounce on the fast-break angle passing lanes, tight openings inside a zone against defensive hands that are held high (most zone defensive coaches advocate hands up), a bounce pass to a cutter who has a ballside position, or a bounce pass on the perimeter to wings or to high posts. The bounce passing changes the timing in relation to other passes.

Good bounce passers must concentrate on increasing their accuracy and quick delivery. They must be careful about the length of their bounce pass. It is a slow pass—takes a longer time from passer to receiver—making it more prone to interceptions. But it has a definite place in fast break basketball.

Players must strengthen their wrist-snap to be ultra-successful with the bounce pass. Weights will do this. Or you can start at 15 feet and gradually move to 30 feet with five minutes or so of practice each day.

All players should learn to step as they pass, and they must learn this early. Also they must learn to take the one-step and pass-off of the dribble-stop. Good players can learn the jump-stop and pass, the one-step and pass, or the skip-stop and pass. The step gives the passer better ball control and balance. He can even stop the pass if the open passing lane suddenly closes. So he must always use two hands. He still has the pivots and his fake passing techniques to help him work the ball.

The one-count skip or shuffle gives you body balance and greater accuracy on your passes. It gives you control which eliminates running over a defender after passing. It also eliminates traveling, which often occurs when a passing lane suddenly closes. Players will not believe the number of bad passes they throw. So you should have your manager record all bad passes, counting the ones that are tagged (touched by a defender but not recovered). By putting that information on the bulletin board daily, players begin to realize their need for better passing. Most of the time the same players make the same mistakes until they see their statistics and begin to count the tags in practice. You should place special emphasis on assists and good plays made by passing. Every player's goal should be: Don't make the same mistake twice; practice the right way and stick to it.

Balance in the air and on the floor is very important for accurate passing. Teaching the details of each skill is essential to the fast break offense, as the ball and the players are moving at double the speed of most patterned-type ball clubs.

Teach the pass receiver to be a "pro outfielder" on every pass. Complete the pass. Ask the passer to take the blame for all pass miscues. This will even out and take the pressure off of the receiver. It also eliminates alibis like "he changed directions," "he has bad hands," etc. But you want some responsibility to be shared by the receiver. This is a delicate coaching maneuver.

The number-one receiving error is the failure to meet every pass hard, especially on the inside post play and wings. Colleges do not have the time to teach passing fundamentals. Weak passing fundamentals will handicap the high school player's chance to play in college. All passing drills must emphasize meeting the pass hard. A good coaching point: concentrate on both ball and player moving as the ball is caught.

Another major passing mistake: allowing the modern defenses to dictate the pass you may use. For example, a player cuts to receive a pass. The defender cuts his direct route to the ball off. So the passer sees the pass receiver running behind the defender, forcing the lob pass, just what the defense intended from the beginning. A step or two left or right of the lob passing lane would allow the passer to use a different pass. Too many forced lobs are intercepted. A dribble by the passer of a few steps in one direction or the other would open a new passing lane. When used correctly the dribble does increase the number of passing lanes available. But again, overuse of the dribble destroys the team fast break.

Secrets of the fast-break overhead pass fundamentals

Your players will be more effective with the overhead pass if they first bring the ball down ready to side-arm, bounce, or baseball pass, and then go up for an overhead pass. From this down position, defenders counter down, then, with a quick upward movement, they can eliminate the telegraphing of this pass. Your player with the ball held overhead can fake left or right before throwing or breaking.

Excellent overhead passers have a quick snap speed in their delivery. A defensive rebounder pivoting on the way down from securing the missed shot can learn to hit an outlet pass receiver near midcourt with a quick snap of the overhead pass.

If you use the overhead pass, you must teach the details. You can use the lower plane passes as counters to the overhead pass. And the blastout dribble technique is a great counter for the defender who is pressed on both sides when he secures the defensive rebound.

The zone defense appreciates having all of your passes thrown from an overhead position. Overhead passes make it easier for them to defend. Against the zone, the bounce pass gets more penetrating assists than the overhead pass.

The overhead pass does allow a little more time for teammates to fake the opponents and open the passing lane as the receiver meets the ball. An overhead pass, without changing planes or faking while in the overhead position, often telegraphs the outlet passing lane before the pass starts. You must not let your players forget the importance of vision in passing the long overhead outlet pass to midcourt. Rebounders who check where the defenders are can fake the overhead to midcourt, pull it back, and hit the original outlet pass receiver on a fly as the defender races to intercept the initial fake of the overhead outlet pass. This overhead fake, along with the fast break defensive guard getting burnt a few times, almost guarantees the overhead pass as a primary outlet pass weapon.

Secrets of practice organization of passing drills

Time is the greatest enemy to overcome in coaching basketball. And when you budget your time more wisely than your opponent, it seems that your next greatest enemy is your own team. So wise budgeting of time and proper execution of the fundamentals lead to more victories than any other two ingredients. The following three-player group drills can be developed into many more. You save time by moving from one skill practice to another without changing the grouping. You can also work several four-player and five-player groupings. You can change the order of the groupings to avoid monotony.

1. Three-player sprint pass drills running in fast break lines (Diagram 2-15).
2. Three-player drill for pass-and-weave (Diagram 2-15).
3. Three-player dribble-and-pass drills (Diagrams 2-13 and 2-15).
4. Three-players with one defender and two players in a passing drill (Diagram 2-12).
5. Three-player triangle rebound-and-pass drill (Diagram 2-15).
6. Three-player rebounder, outlet, center lane cutter drill (Diagram 2-14).
7. Three-player wing pass into high post with defender on wing and a defender on post (Diagrams 2-16, 2-17, and 2-18).
8. Three players plus three defenders double guard high post drill (Diagrams 2-16, 2-17, and 2-18).

After the drill practices, have all the players run the entire fast break at half speed. On the transition you first must be sure the passers enjoy mechanical success. Then you start the final step by moving up to game tempo. You want to be sure all the players understand all the options. After racing at game tempo for a few days, you add defensive pressure according to the player's experience. From then on you want to keep all of your drills at game tempo even if you need to shorten the time allocated. Should a player's fundamentals retrogress, you might go back to the drills at half speed for a minute or so. You might even go back to single purpose drills until the forgotten skills have advanced again to an acceptable level.

The popular bull-in-a-ring drill emphasizes the fake before passing. You execute it with six players in the free-throw and center circles. If a pass is tagged or intercepted, the passer becomes the bull. Passing, by a stationary opponent whose hands are active, helps to develop the passing skill with head, shoulder, and eye fakes. When the execution is good, you advance to three passes against three defenders with keep-away passing. This covers about a quarter of the court. You may expand it to half court. You can even call out the pass to be used: hand-off, shoulder baseball pass, chest pass, side arm pass, bounce pass, and underhand pass or overhead pass.

Secrets to using the hook pass

The hook pass was purposely left out in order to place it in a specific situation. The hook pass has the longest telegraphed time, but it can be used by the rebounder who makes long, clear pass-outs or for high jump pass situations.

For some reason certain players who learn to hook pass early will use it in close passing situations. This motion is a telegraphed pass that defenders can read and intercept. You should keep the hook pass for long pass situations when your players are relatively free from defensive pressure.

At every opportunity in all passing drills, you should demand a head-and-shoulder fake before the pass, and the fake should be away from the passing lane the passer intends to use. But don't spare the discipline of the quick, accurate pass release. The quick release passer never looks hard and long at the passing lane to be used. The quick release pass also eliminates cocking of the ball before the pass starts.

Passers must learn to keep their eyes on the hands of the receiver. The defender cannot read the passer's eyes even when they are on low targets or the floor. Good passers learn to read their teammates' moves, thereby knowing early which passing lane will be open. A good passer may look one way while moving in the opposite direction; but once he delivers the pass, he should see the ball all the way into the receiver's hands.

Fast-break passing drills

Your fast-break passing drills should simulate your fast break patterns. In other words, after your players have learned the basic passing fundamentals and you are comfortable with their execution, your drills should not only teach passing but also teach the options of your basic fast break movement.

Diagram 2-12 displays a rebounder throwing the overhead pass to an outlet pass receiver. These two throw a chest pass on a trip down the floor. You can add a defender if you like. This would force players 2 and 5 to dribble once before passing or risk an interception. This adds passing judgment to the drill. You can also use the chest, baseball, overhead, and bounce passes in this drill. Players move at a controlled speed. The drill teaches the quick catch and release. As players move straight down court, they turn at the waist to receive and pass. You can vary the distance between players to increase the wrist-snap which adds ball speed. As passers move down the floor, you require them to push off from the outside foot.

Diagram 2-13 exhibits the dribble direction change upon receiving the pass. This is required while running the break if the passing lane is defended. The passer should break hard down court to get ahead of the dribbler, forcing defensive adjustments. The receiver must angle in to

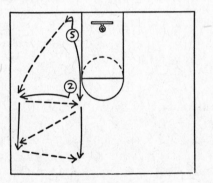

Diagram 2-12

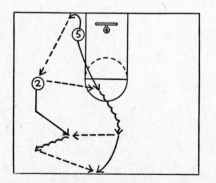

Diagram 2-13

receive the pass. A key to watch out for: the side lane passers who move in towards the court center instead of staying wide.

Diagram 2-14 illustrates the third player being added to the break: two long rebounders teaming with a board rebounder. This calls for various passes: the outlet overhead, the long baseball, the chest, the bounce. And if you add a defender or two, the dribble will have to come into play. Side lane cutters must stay wide until they reach the top of the key. Player movement away from the straight line break is a lane changing run. You can add the lane changing runs after you have taught them. This adds options to your fast break. And we will add fast break drills with four and five players later after we have shown the complete break with all of its options, including the lane changing runs.

Diagram 2-15 is the typical 3-on-2 break. Three players speed in a straight line against two defenders. Here you begin teaching how teams will defense your fast break: the two defenders parallel or in a tandem.

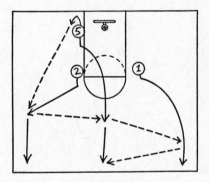

Diagram 2-14

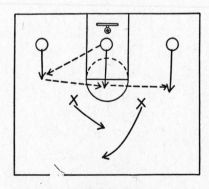

Diagram 2-15

Diagram 2-16 shows a passing drill at the end of the break. This leads into the secondary phase of the break, presented in Chapter 7. Player 1 dribbles across the floor. He executes a jump-stop-reverse pass to a trailer, player 2, who hits the high post, player 5. Both players 1 and 2 cut around the post. Diagrams 2-17 and 2-18 exhibit two other possible cutting options. Diagram 2-18 shows both cutters going over the same side. Diagram 2-17 displays both cutters using a downcourt straight cut. You add two defenders and you are teaching parts of your secondary break.

Diagram 2-19 displays another secondary option of the break. Player 3 passes to player 2 and cuts on a give-and-go to the basket.

Diagram 2-20 reveals the ending of four players in the break. Player 4 is a trailer. Player 3 hits player 1 at the wing. Player 1 immediately hits the trailer, player 4. Player 4 must time his arrival. He receives a pass from the wing. But the wing may fake-drive, then pass; or the wing and player 3 may work and give-and-go; or player 4 might even pass back to

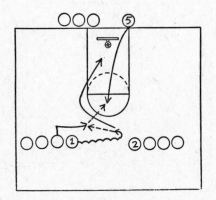

Diagram 2-16

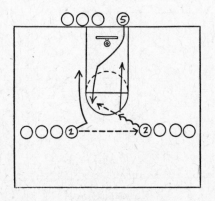

Diagram 2-17

player 1 and go post up low; or player 4 could pass to the center lane cutter, player 3, who can reverse the ball to the other side, shoot, or even bring the pass back to player 1. All of these options will be covered when we explain the secondary phase of the fast break in Chapter 7.

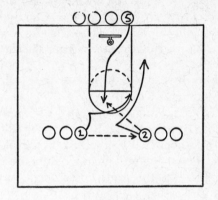

Diagram 2-18

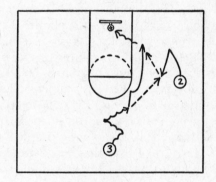

Diagram 2-19

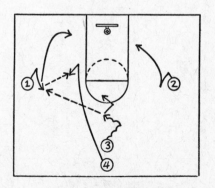

Diagram 2-20

From Diagrams 2-12 through 2-20 you should see how the break develops its many options. You can see passing drills which not only teach the passing skills necessary for success but also teach the basic movements and options of the fast break itself. You can even invent more passing and rebounding drills which provide instruction on the full break. The success of your break depends upon your imagination. By adding defenders, you force your passers to use passing judgments. But don't teach passing judgment until passing skills are well learned.

Passing drills to develop center lane passing skills

Getting the ball to the center of the court, whether by dribble or by pass, is the essence of fast break basketball. Diagrams 2-21 through 2-28 display many ways of accomplishing the fast break with the ball in the middle lane. Each can be made into a drill. There are many other possibilities. Your imagination is the limit. These diagrams reveal the many options of the basic fast break.

Diagrams 2-21 and 2-22 exhibit player 3 getting the defensive rebound. What he does with the ball depends on the defense he sees. His passing judgment is extremely important. In Diagram 2-21, player 3 blasts out with a dribble because he sees players 1 and 2 covered, eliminating the outlet pass to midcourt. As player 3 blasts out, the defender on player 1 slides over to stop player 3. Player 3 immediately passes to player 1. On the other hand, Diagram 2-22 shows player 1 open for the outlet pass from player 3. Player 4 immediately fills the middle lane (which you will find out is player 4's responsibility).

Diagrams 2-23 through 2-27 demonstrate possible passing lanes when player 5 rebounds and throws an outlet pass. Of course, player 5 also has the blastout as a possibility. Diagram 2-23 is the basic break outlet pass to player 2 who hits player 3 in the middle lane immediately.

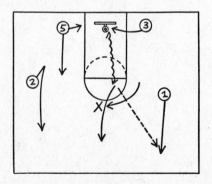

Diagram 2-21

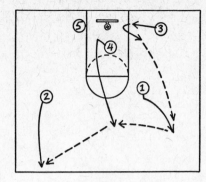

Diagram 2-22

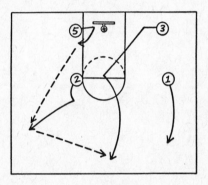

Diagram 2-23

In Diagram 2-24, the outlet pass to player 2 is defended. Player 3 cuts back to player 5 for the outlet pass, and the break is on its way. In Diagram 2-25, player 2 receives the outlet pass from Player 5 and checks player 3 in the middle lane. Player 3 is defensed. Player 3 continues to run his fly which clears the middle lane. Player 2 passes to player 1 who has raced down the opposite sideline. Because player 3 continued to run, he was in an excellent position to receive the pass-back from player 1, and the break continued. Player 2 had other options he could have used before passing to player 1. However player 2 should pass to player 1 if player 1 is ahead of the ball and open. But let's say player 1 is not open and neither is player 3. Then player 2 should dribble to the middle and exchange lanes with player 3, putting player 1 in the right lane, player 2 in the middle lane, and player 3 in the left lane. On the other hand, players 1, 2, and 3 might sometimes face three defenders. Diagram 2-26 illustrates one possibility when this happens. Player 3 drives toward the basket and player 2 cuts behind player 3 for a hand-off pass. Players 2 and 3 exchange lanes. Player 2 can pass to player 1, and they can exchange lanes. Diagram 2-27 shows another possibility when players 1, 2, and 3 face three defenders. If player 1 cuts in front of his defender, although he is ahead of the ball, player 3 can hit player 1 and players 1 and 3 would exchange lanes.

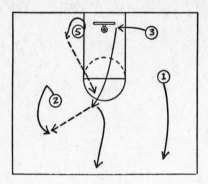

Diagram 2-24

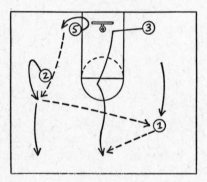

Diagram 2-25

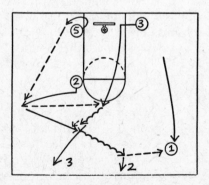

Diagram 2-26

Diagram 2-28 displays yet another option. Player 4 rebounds and outlet passes to player 2. Player 1 races to the center lane, receiving a pass from player 2. Player 3 fills player 1's usual lane. (You will find this is a regular player lane exchange rule.)

Regardless of the drills you make up, you want to begin with just passing. Then advance to running the break with no defenders. Gradually you add the defensive roadblocks which require passing judgments to circumvent.

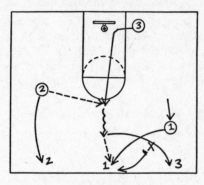

Diagram 2-27

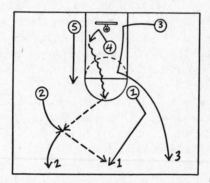

Diagram 2-28

Summary of fast break success based on passing skills

1. The fast break demands a positive running attitude, and it requires a disciplined concentration toward learning the fast-moving passing skills.

2. You must offer fast break options over the entire playing court which will counter defensive roadblocks whenever they may occur. Shifting lane cutters help to create new passing lanes which will help avoid these defensive roadblocks.

3. Fast break conditioning can be accomplished as your team covers all fast break options. Tired passers will turn the ball over with poor passing techniques.

4. Fast break success depends on board control throughout the game, and on throwing pass strikes to cutting teammates.

5. Fast-break advancing ball ability depends upon team passing plus quick, good passing judgments.

6. Fast break offenses should push the game tempo beyond the ability of the opponents to counter over the four quarters.

7. Successful fast break offenses come from a total commitment on every fast break opportunity—held balls, tips, free-throw line, out-of-bounds, interceptions, made and missed baskets. The total commitment never stops—the team moves from primary break into a secondary break into a half-court set offense. The defense never stops the break; only your players can.

8. Fast break adds a big plus to all phases of the game tempo.

9. Fast break adds to a good defensive tempo by setting a stronger tempo.

The first team drill for fast break passing should cover all the details of early fundamentals used to learn the different passes and their execution.

You start with two fast break players, 18 to 20 feet apart, running full court. Discipline them to concentrate on carrying their arms high, turning at the hips for the catch and the pass. Shuffle step running is made with both feet off of the floor as the player receives the pass. The passes should be delivered quickly and accurately, shoulder high. Slow passes will be fumbled more than fast passes. The receiver must reach for the pass with his elbows flexed, the heels of his hands fairly close together, and fingers cupped. You cannot ask a tall boy to run and catch a ball thrown below his hips. Passes below shoulder height to quick cutters usually are fumbled, turned-over.

Some coaches may think the shuffle step slows the break. It should be a quick skip at full speed, thus giving the player balance for a second to make the pass, to dribble, to use a change of pace, or to stop. If you vary the distance separating the two running players, you will develop arm strength for accurate longer passes.

The two outlet pass receivers should break wide from their deep rebound positions. These side lane cutters should stay wide, 15 to 20 feet ahead of the center lane cutter, who is cutting down court to score or pass.

If the center lane cutter takes the ball past the free-throw lane, he should jump, shoot, pass, or go all the way for the lay-up. He could stop and fake the jumper at the free-throw area and counter with a pass to any moving, open teammate near the basket. If the center lane cutter is inexperienced, you may want an ironclad rule: stop at the free-throw line—if you go below the line you must drive all the way without passing. However, it is best to allow the middle cutter, your best athlete, all the above options.

The most important steps to take to develop a successful fast break offense will come through the constant use of game condition drills. You can teach rebounding, passing, and the options of your break by using the same drills.

The players may have gone through the preliminary drills mechanically, but in game situations they don't show any ability to execute the desired passes. Skill and confidence seem to be missing. You, as coach, can wait until the passer sees the open passing lane and puts his judgment passing on the line. Or you can go back to the learning drills and utilize game condition pressure against the passer.

Newly learned mechanical pass skills may not hold against the first game pressure. The player may revert to old habits unless the new skills are overlearned. The passer needs to practice using the right pass for a specific situation under defensive pressure.

You can set up a drill to practice just the weak pass skill. You can take the drills from your basic pattern or from a fast break move. You can lift a part of the break out that shows a definite weakness. You begin by applying medium pressure against completing the passes. Then you add your game pressure again.

You can break down your complete basic break into parts, such as the outlet pass, passing to the center lane cutter, center lane cutter to the weakside wing, rebounder to the center lane cutter, rebounder to a deep-side lane cutter, and so forth. You can even consider all of the rebounder's options before considering all of the outlet receiver's options, etc. You might scrimmage for a long time without a specific weak situation showing, or visible only once or twice. But by using drills your players' skills will develop many times faster than if you just scrimmage.

If you are fortunate enough to have four to six baskets in your gym, make specific pass practice assignments for each pass you wish to drill. Or one basket could be for all the options of the rebounder, the next basket for all the options of the outlet receiver, etc. Five minutes or less will give the player concentrated practice on his weakness. You drill for perfection, even though you have to take learning steps to get there.

Coaches should always help the player by pointing out his successes. This helps him to gain confidence and it prepares the player to concentrate on eliminating his skill weaknesses.

Your basketball bulletin board should help emphasize the harmful place that the loss of the ball has in winning a game. It should hold a daily place in your plans, not just on game statistics. If you will emphasize the following 15 points on alternate days in practice, your passing skills will reach championship caliber.

1. Floor and air balance are essential to accurate passing.
2. Pass and hit the open spot on the receiver.
3. Each pass that is used must have proper execution.
4. Pass and receive the ball with the fingers, not the palms.
5. Eliminate the hard look at the passing lane before passing.
6. Look down but on the target.
7. Good pass judgment needed for each situation.
8. Fake ahead of the pass to eliminate the telegraph.
9. Protect the ball at all times.
10. Keep the ball in motion. A still ball is easy to tag.
11. If the dribble is a pass, protect it all the time.
12. Pass so that the receiver meets the pass.
13. A quick release of the pass eliminates a telegraph.
14. To eliminate turnovers accuracy should be the prime objective.
15. Always have an alternate pass or movement available to keep defensive pressure off of the ball.

Secrets of the Dribbling Fast Breaks

Our fast break emphasizes passing, using options to always have a running lane open. But there are variations to this fast break which involve dribbling. Dribbling can also occur within the basic break itself.

Under the chapter on variations the dribble break will be dealt with as a secondary option movement in the total fast break philosophy. You want to take advantage of every superior skill that can advance the ball on the fast break without finding yourself in one camp or the other. Passing skill is the number-one fast break philosophy; but the dribble under control is a good second.

If your team has a speed advantage over the opposition, the fast break will magnify this advantage in comparison to the patterned quarter-court attack. The dribble can be an asset to the break, or it can destroy the team play of your fast break.

There is no dribbler nor runner who can move faster than a pass. The 1-on-1 dribble habit of giving up the ball only when in trouble has to be recycled by the coach. The two earliest learned skills are shooting and dribbling. Too much of either by any one individual will quickly spoil your team.

The misuses of the dribble are several and should be clearly understood by each player. The learning emphasis should be placed on uses that help the team attack, not for individual fulfillment. A dribble can advance the ball when all passing lanes are closed. A player can use the dribble to escape trouble, to drive for the lay-up when there is an opening, and to pull defenses out where the offense wants them.

The major negative use of the dribble is when a player refuses to pass to an open player ahead of the ball. Dribbling from a personal view will never be tolerated. Dribbling that allows the defense to get ballside defense positions must be criticized and refuted. Dribbling without looking down court for an open teammate will quickly destroy your fast break. Dribbling for a shot with a wide-open teammate closer to the basket is never condoned. Dribbling which allows the defense to double-team the ball and create a turnover must be severely rebuffed.

However, the dribbler can be the sixth player on the floor for the good fast break teams. Two quick dribbles, left or right, force the defense to change positions on their opponents as the center cutter races down floor with the ball. The dribble followed by a quick pass-off is harder to defend against (no telegraphing) if the dribbler is under control. The blastout from rebounding frequently leaves one or two fast break defenders behind.

Granted, the dribble break is slower, but a good dribbler can add to the fast break if he never lets the defense stack up against the ball. A center cutter, for example, who is able to feed and shoot well from the top of the key, backed by the threat of his drive to the basket, cannot be replaced in the fast break scheme by any other type of player.

As a coach you must never allow any contest between passing and dribbling. Passing is the number-one skill in fast-break basketball offenses. But the good dribbler has a place in fast break basketball and they must be made aware of their spots for contributions. Passing and dribbling is one of those many areas where you as coach have a direct say in your season's success.

Never allow sloppy execution to slip into your fast-break passing or dribbling drills. You can always stop the drill and begin again later. Players play as they drill.

It pays to be skillful with one pass rather than sloppy with three or four. It also pays to have one good dribbling maneuver than to have several mediocre ones. Learning one pass or dribble maneuver well before trying to execute another leads to fast-break and individual successes.

Summary

Before drilling the full-court fast break you should use the 2-on-2, the 3-on-3, and the 4-on-4 drills. The keep-away drills also help in the development of pass judgments. You can cut the passing area to a quarter of the court with emphasis on accuracy which adds more pressure to passing. You can, after a few days of only passing, permit the players to dribble out of trouble. All offensive players must move to fake their opponent away from a teammate who will pass to them. This teaches eyes up. Also, teammates must move away from the dribbler who is moving toward them so there will be no double-teaming by the defense. Players must hit the teammate when open and breaking for the pass. This eliminates someone controlling the dribble. When a player dribbles and a teammate is open, you must stop the drill and point out the open player. Faking the opponent away from the dribble or away from the passing lane is called setting up the opponent. Emphasize jump-stops before passing. Balance is essential for accurate passing off of the dribble. The jump-stop gives you this balance. The careless use of the pivot or the fake-and-dribble will cost teams turnovers. Always know where the defenders are before pivoting and beginning a dribble.

Passer's eyes should look away from the passing lane to be used, but they must always see their teammate's hand signaling for the pass. The ball should be faked well at times before passing. This helps to keep the passing lanes open. Players must also learn the quick pass right off of the catch.

Secrets of Fast Break Shooting

There are two types of shots which develop from the fast break: the driving lay-up at the end of the break, and the explosive jump shot when the lane to the basket is closed. Some other shots can come off of the break, the hook by a post man cutting down the center lane for example, but the primary two are the jumper and the lay-up.

Coaches all recognize that good shooting requires special mechanical discipline for every shot. Each shot has a rhythm of its own. The difficulty in gaining shooting efficiency comes from players who try to put their ego mark of individuality on the shot delivery. They mess up good, consistent shooting which comes from establishing a smooth shooting rhythm.

Coaches sometimes are reluctant to make changes, and they leave the shot alone even when the shooter hits only occasionally. Some children start on a 10-foot-high basket with regular weighted basketballs. Because these youngsters must throw the ball instead of shooting it, they develop bad mechanical habits. They disrupt their smooth shooting rhythm.

Many lay-ups should result from fast break basketball. Yet many players shoot their lay-ups just over the rim. This habit of just getting the ball over the iron reduces the chances of success. A coach should require his players to lay the ball high on the board. The high lay-up cools down the moving ball speed and gives the ball a chance to drop in for a score.

It is very hard for players to develop the confidence necessary to break old habits. But the coach should try to break the habit in the lay-up and the jump shot. While traveling at 12 miles an hour, your arm action should be lifting and bringing the arm back to soften the ball on the board. Players driving hard to the basket sometimes push the ball at the basket too hard.

Fast break shooting from the floor needs much greater discipline in order to control the shot balance because the shooter moves into shooting position at a great speed. Only fundamentally sound shots will succeed under great defensive pressure at great speed.

Have you had your team get shaky from the opponent's pressure, or was it intimidated by hot floor shooting? You may find your team walks up to the free-throw line and brings the floor intimidation with it. Players shoot a poor percentage until they settle down. This happens to good shooters too. Some players bring their snap jump shots to the free throw line, because it has given them an average of 40 to 50 percent success in floor shooting. Have them stick to the slow, flexed, nicely arched free-throw shot. Don't let them use the first shot as a guide for concentration, and then use a slow rhythm for a second shot that hits.

Try using the jump-stop with the body flexed and the feet close. The foot on the side of the shot arm should lead slightly. You may want your right foot to lead while going down the right lane and your left foot to lead when shooting on the run down the left side lane. This not only gives you better balance, it enables you to get the shot off just a fraction of a second quicker. Have the weight on the forward foot. The shot starts from the ankle through the leg, hip, and right (or left) side of the body, with the arm and hand in a straight line. The shoulder, arm, elbow, and wrist follow in this straight line with a swan neck finish of the wrist, and a follow-through that puts some reverse English on the ball. Shooters should hit the floor 6 or 8 inches ahead of their take-off spot, especially when they receive the ball and shoot when moving at great great speeds.

The lift from the legs should create the same height to the shooting platform each time. There should be no break in the rhythm of the shot. The fake should free the player for his shot if he is closely guarded. How high he jumps should always be consistent—shooters should not jump higher just because they are closely guarded. The point of release should be at the same height each time. The legs propel the shot, which is arched to a specific point, with hand and arm as the guide in the delivery. This form allows perfect relaxation of the upper body. The arch on the shot depends upon the distance to the basket. Small players will get more nonpressured shots by lifting all shots. The player's shoulders while on the shot platform should be square to the basket. Turning one's shoulders is an error found in many shooters, especially when they are moving on an angle and not straight at the basket. A lack of follow-through is another error. Arm tension, moving off balance, and breaking the shot rhythm creates percentage shooting problems.

Spot shooting on the fast break's most likely opportunities for non-pressured shots is a good drill. In practice try to spot-shoot on a circle, making every shot the same length to develop the muscle and shot lifting skill habit. Some shooters have an arch problem, that of adjusting the apex of the shot arch halfway between shooter and basket. Start close to the basket, lift the shot high, step back 3 or 4 feet, lift the shot with an arch, continue until the good percentage limit is reached.

The problem of shots moving left or right from off the center may be due to body or ankle weaving as shooters leave the floor. The greater the speed when receiving the ball the better the chance the player will continue to move in the direction of the shot. Try having the shooter shoot at a mark the size of a dollar, about 12 feet up on the wall, while standing 15 to 20 feet away. Then have the player race to the same spot and make the same shot. This shooting drill can get immediate concentration. Let the good mechanics do the shooting, and try for five straight hits. Your better shooters can use this same technique by shooting without hitting the rim. By doing this drill several times the shooting should straighten out. The fall-away shots, the wrist-snap flat shots, and the hesitation hang shots must also be corrected. Watch some high school teams during warm-ups and you will see players practicing all kinds of deliveries they have seen the pros use; but during the game, when it counts, they fail to make even the easy lay-up shots.

If you stay with it and teach good form, your offense will give you a stable return. Remember that good percentage shots can balance off a lot of miscues and turnovers. No matter how perfect you run your fast break, it does not count until the shooter delivers.

You want all of your fast-break shooting drills to incorporate a run before a shot. This teaches balance before shooting. It also conditions. Your drills can incorporate the lanes you would like each player to learn.

Diagram 2-29 shows player 3 passing to player 1. Player 1 dribbles a step or so before shooting his jump shot. Player 1 wants to stop on his right foot letting his left foot be his lead foot, slightly in front of his right foot. This is a much quicker stop than if he used his right foot as the lead foot. The opposite footwork should occur on the other side of the floor. Player 3 and 1 would exchange positions so both could drill at shooting on balance from the left side lane off a feed from a center cutter. Both player 3 and player 1 will run the outside lanes as well as the center lanes.

Diagram 2-30 displays a shooting drill for the big men, rebounders 4 and 5. Player 3 dribbles down the middle lane, passing to outside left sidelane player 2. Player 4 streaks down the middle lane. Player 2 can hit

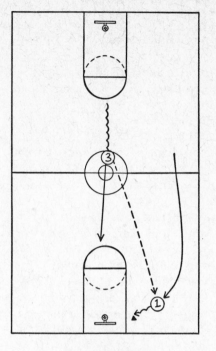

Diagram 2-29

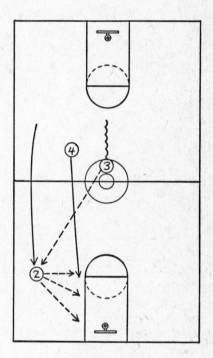

Diagram 2-30

player 4 as he races down the key. Player 4 must be on balance expecting the pass. Player 4 can take this pass on in for a lay-up; or he can receive the ball at the midpost area, requiring player 4 to take a turnaround jumper or to spin back into the middle of the court. Player 2 could elect to hit player 4 at the middle of the court key area or at the high post, but his greatest percentage shot would come from the low post area. This low post positioning would require player 4 to know how to operate from the low post position.

All fast-break shooting drills must require motion before the shooting action. Standing and shooting can be good practice for form, but speed shooting is required for the fast breaking offense.

Mathematical Principles of Fast Break Basketball

The number of shots the fast break team should take ranges between 60 and 75. Fast break attacks should have the 15-foot jump shots perfected. They should have the power to penetrate the defense and get inside the 15-foot area for nonpressured shots. Of those 60 to 75 shots, 40 to 50 should be inside the 60 percent area and under 20 outside the 40 percent area. This would give your team about 50 points, plus 12 free throws, thus making 60 to 70 points. That is enough points to win the majority of your games, providing your defense can hold your opponents to 50 shots plus ten free throws.

The turnovers range also plays an important part. Be sure to emphasize the battle of the turnovers. Your defense can force turnovers and your offense can cut down on an opponent's turnovers. Your defense can turn opposing teams' turnovers into fast break lay-ups. By eliminating your offensive turnovers, you reduce the number of easy fast break lay-ups by your opponents. You have to make your team very aware of these mathematical points. You should emphasize this in every practice and on your bulletin board. You must commend every improvement. Make your players aware that turnovers play a big part in winning games. Every turnover could take away one of the breaks-made shots, and give your opponents an easy shot.

The free-throw scoring difference can be the deciding factor. Game after game shows that field goals are about equal with free throws to decide a number of games. Away from the home court, the difference between man-to-man and zone can be crucial. Being behind several times in a game has a bearing on who makes the most fouls.

Relationship Between Turnovers and Fast Break Basketball

To some players the loss of the ball does not have any real meaning. For the most part, small details of ball handling have not become a solid habit to them. If high school teams turn the ball over from 20 to 30 times, the turnover rate becomes a major negative factor in winning games. To cut down turnovers by 50 percent becomes a game winning goal.

Some fast break teams, relying on the opposition to make turnovers right back, call it an even trade—and therefore not instrumental in the outcome of the game. Granted fast break teams turn the ball over more than ball control teams, but you should never cease trying to improve your execution. Fast break tempo and turnovers are not synonymous terms.

Work and concentration on the fundamental ball handling skills will score big points, sometimes as many points as you will get at the free-throw line. You must emphasize better ball control when you begin developing your fast break offense. The way to eliminate a turnover problem is to take the time to teach skill first, then discipline the player's execution of the skill until the moves are mastered.

Coaches could use twice the practice time they allot themselves. But time is not the answer for giving the opposition 8 to 15 more shots. High school coaches blessed with lower-grade-school teams that have been coached by sound fundamentalists inherit a terrific advantage over other coaches whose new recruits did not have the benefit of early skill training. A review of some of your past lost ball situations should reinforce the position of good ball handling in daily lesson plans.

SECRETS OF DEVELOPING
THE BASIC FAST BREAK

A fast break team's rebounding is based upon gaining the five best rebound positions to give rebounders the opportunity to control the boards. The three under-the-basket rebounders form a team triangle that covers the sides and front of the basket. The triangle rebounders must get the inside position and block out the opponent's board pressure. This should eliminate the second or third shot and create the starting move of the break. The two guards or wings occupy positions near the corner of the free-throw lines and are called the deep rebounders. They are responsible for long rebounds and receiving the outlet pass.

Four steps, each taught as a separate entity, evolve from all fast breaks: getting the ball (mostly by rebounding), outlet passing, lane filling, and finishing up (mostly lay-ups). To be an accomplished fast break team, you must control the boards. And more importantly you must adopt a fast break attitude. Your guards and wings should have the desire to take the ball up the defense's tailbones. They must commit themselves to never walking the ball up the court. They must never concede that the fast break will not work on any one possession.

Basic Principles of the Fast Break

These are the ten basic rules or axioms of the basic break. These are the things you are going to do every possession. When you have accomplished these ten duties, your fast break is assured:

1. Block out and get the rebound. You cannot be a fast break team without good rebounding.
2. Quick and long outlet passes—to somewhere near the ten-second line. Use the blast-out technique only as a last resort.
3. Get the outlet pass to a wingman. If one is not there, pass to the middle man.
4. Wingmen should stay wide, about 3 feet from out-of-bounds, until they reach the free-throw line, then cut sharply to the basket.
5. Use the middle man, especially from midcourt to the basket. The center lane cutter can dribble in this case and force the defense to declare itself.
6. If the middle is jammed, take the ball down the side lane. These two wingmen can race ahead of the ball in a 2-on-1 situation.
7. Wingmen must not arrive at the basket simultaneously.
8. The middle man must stop at the foul line unless he is going all the way on a dribble for the score.
9. Wingmen do not cross under the basket.
10. A secondary break follows the primary break without any delay, resetting, or hesitating.

Basic Fast-Break Starting Movement and Drills

Diagram 3-1 displays the basic fast break. In the following sections we will diagram and explain the options of the basic break in detail.

This approach will familiarize the reader with each player's position on the basic break. Diagram 3-1 shows player movements in advancing the break from one end of the floor to the other. Some fast-break advancing speed comes from players who get into related positions down court.

Fast break speed will be improved further by eliminating as much dribbling as possible. One or two dribbles may open the passing lanes without losing speed, but each player must give up the ball to any teammate ahead of him. Player 1, the guard away from the rebounding side, races as deep as possible. He, in effect, runs a fly pattern. Player 2 should flash to the outlet side lane position, going deep out beyond the head of the key, putting his back to the sideline. This way player 2 can see the entire court. Player 3 cuts down the center lane with player 4 trailing and ready to put added pressure on the defense if it tries to gang up on the fast break at any point. Player 5, the rebounder, trails the entire break.

Drills showing the outlet receiver's options

The outlet receiver is the first player to receive the pass from the rebounder. He has several options available to him which defeat any defensive attempts to stop the fast break.

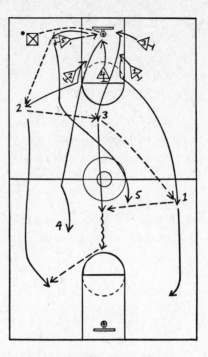

Diagram 3-1

a. The long pass option (Diagram 3-2)

Procedure:

1. Line players up as shown, making sure all the players who will play a particular position get to drill at those positions.
2. Player 5 rebounds the missed shot.
3. Player 2 flashes out to the outlet receiving position. Meanwhile player 1 has gone on his fly pattern.
4. When player 2 receives the outlet pass, he checks the defense so he can make the proper judgment for his next pass. In Diagram 3-2 player 2 decides to hit player 1 on the fly pattern. He could have hit player 3 who could have passed to player 1.
5. The drill continues with the three players running the fast break against two waiting defenders.

Objectives:

1. To teach passing judgment by the outlet pass receiver.
2. To teach the 3-on-2 fast break.
3. To teach the options of the basic fast break.

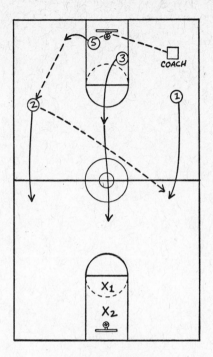

Diagram 3-2

b. The lane changing option (Diagram 3-3)

Procedure:

1. Line the players up as shown, making sure each player gets to play each position he could be responsible for.

2. When player 2 receives the outlet pass from player 5, he sees player 1 cutting to the center lane. When player 3 sees player 1 taking the duties of the center lane, it is his responsibility to assume the responsibility of the lane vacated by player 1.

3. Player 2 hits player 1 who passes to player 3, and the break continues against the two waiting defenders.

4. This gives the basic break a different arrival grouping. Player 1 should arrive before either wingman. Player 3 should arrive just ahead of player 2.

Objectives:

1. To teach passing judgment by the outlet pass receiver.

2. To teach the 3-on-2 fast break.

3. To teach the options of the basic break.

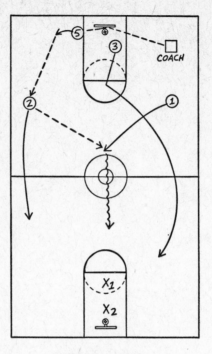

Diagram 3-3

c. The dribble option (Diagram 3-4)

Procedure:

1. Line the players up as shown, making sure each player gets to play all the positions he will be responsible for.
2. When player 2, the outlet receiver, receives the pass from the rebounder, player 5, he sees that the center lane cutter, player 3, is defensed. Player 3 goes on the fly or cuts to the sideline. If player 3 continued on the fly, it would cue player 4 to take the center lane. If player 2 wishes, he could pass to player 4 and reverse the ball to the fly pattern being run by player 1. Player 2 could hit player 3 as he cuts to the sideline—this is the sideline fast break, covered in Chapter 6. Or player 2 could take the ball to the middle lane by dribbling (Diagram 3-4).
3. These three continue their attack on the two awaiting defenders.

Objectives:

1. To teach passing judgment by the outlet pass receiver.
2. To teach the 3-on-2 fast break.
3. To teach the options of the basic break.

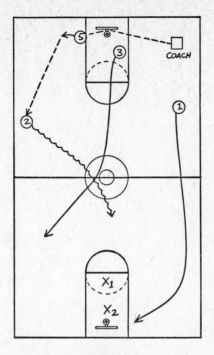

Diagram 3-4

These four Diagrams (3-1 through 3-4) illustrate some options which are available to circumvent any defensive roadblocks which might try to stop the basic break. Chapter 4 covers all the possible options available at all the positions. These drills were offered here so you could have a better understanding of the basic break. Good judgment can be taught by such drills; players are not born with such basketball savvy.

Diagram 3-5 illustrates the multiple fast-break conditioning run drill. The purpose of this drill is to make sure all the players know the basic cuts of the basic break before you begin teaching the possible options. You simply run the break down the floor, realign the people, and run the break back up the floor. Your manager or assistant coach can shoot at one end of the floor while you shoot at the other. After you have assigned who will take the ball out, you can even include the basic break after made baskets. The emphasis is on controlled tempo, accurate downcourt passing, correct lane choices, and accurate outlet passing from the rebounders.

You can call for a specific pass to be used, such as a chest or bounce pass for passing out on the floor, the baseball shoulder pass if the shot is made, and a two-handed overhead pass on outlet passes from a rebound. After teaching the options, you can even call which option you want the team to run. You can use this same dummy drill to teach alternate lane cutting.

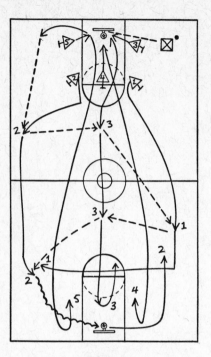

Diagram 3-5

Diagram 3-1 and Diagram 3-5 are introductory fast-break multiple runs without detailed emphasis on how you are to achieve the final goal. Of course, those details are what enable you to enjoy success with your break. The fundamental details were presented in Chapter 2; and the optional details are in Chapter 4.

Diagram 3-5 shows side lane cutters changing sides at the end of the break. This is to allow continuous running of the form break. Dribbler 2 takes a shot, goes under the basket, and takes over the opposite lane. The nonshooter, player 1, cuts across the key at the free-throw line and takes over the opposite lane. Player 3 assumes the center position and can go in either direction. Players 4 and 5 come down to rebound or to get into the secondary phase of the fast break (see Chapter 7). You can include the secondary phase in this running exercise after you have taught it. You can require player 2 or 1 to take the jump shot. When made, you run your break after a made basket; when missed, you rebound and go in the other direction with your basic break. This insures the break is run continuously without a coach having to touch the ball. For maximum conditioning each crew should run the break 16 times before you change the crews.

Secrets of the Two Rebounding Fast Break Concepts

Today's passing game offenses, slow-down strategies, and spread patterned offenses frequently will remove your 3, 4, and 5 players from their primary rebounding positions. If you play man-to-man defense, a motion offense, for example, could take the two outlet pass receivers to the corner and pull out the best rebounders to the perimeter before a shot is taken. When you intend to run the man-to-man defense, you have to decide if you want your players to hurry to their standard rebound positions or memorize and know all positions, so the break can continue regardless of the defense you intend to play. Triangle rebounders and deep rebounders should practice racing to a rebound position as the shot starts up if you choose this as your rebounding concept for your fast break. All players should learn all positions if that becomes your break concept. Regardless of which concept (boxing out and running from where you are, or racing to your normal assigned rebound positions) you intend to use, the transition from defense to the offensive break rebound position is difficult. It should be practiced continually. Practicing against attacks which will change your rebound-fast break positioning will convert that weakness into a strength.

If you play zone your players are already in proper rebound position. If you play man-to-man and block off, then fill the nearest lane— because you taught each player all the positions, you are really never out of rebound-fast break position. A real problem presents itself when you want your three big rebounders, especially players 4 and 5, to always get back to their original or comparable board position. You may think you will never need this strategy, but someday you may find yourself with two exceptionally tall and talented rebounders who cannot handle the ball out on the open floor. With that in mind, the following sections will show ways of getting at least two rebounders back into the rebound triangle.

Regardless of the type of offense used, most offensive teams have designated three specific players to go to the offensive boards. You should assign your three rebounders the opponent's three offensive rebounders. The offensive rebounders start moving to the boards as the shot goes up. Your defensive board people block off then race to inside rebound position.

Switching man-to-man defense is another counter if the height and speed of your defenders are comparable. You may counter with a strategy similar to the matching zone. This switching on all crossing of personnel will keep your better rebounders at home, but it may end as the shot goes up with your rebounders not guarding their offensive rebounders.

Whoever is assigned to a jump shooter 12 feet or further from the boards should not crash the defensive boards. This defender on the jump shooter can become player 1 in our fast break system. This defender, in other words, runs the fly pattern. The jump shooter must go back on defense because he cannot get to the board on time; and, if he does not go back, the fly pattern will give the fast break a lay-up. This strategy will disrupt the offensive board strategy of the opponents.

Two different offensive patterns are shown in Diagrams 3-6 and 3-7 which catch the fast break rebounders away from the basket. Your rebounders hustle to a quick recovery position, then on with the fast break.

Diagram 3-6 illustrates an offensive move that forces the defense out of the balanced triangle rebound position. The end of the offensive attack is shown; the beginning position of the fast break as the shot is taken is also depicted. X4 is caught out on the perimeter as the shot goes up. But you do not want X4 becoming the fly man on your break, you do not want X4 in the three-lane frontal attack. X4, therefore, must go to his rebound position even if his man had taken the shot.

Player 2 is underneath as the shot goes up, and he stays to rebound. You never want to leave a weak side underneath rebound position. It is better to lose the break than to give up this primary rebounding position. Player 1 is caught on the baseline weakside court position. Player 1 flashes to a long rebound position, then out to receive the outlet pass. Player 3 presses the shooter and goes on the fly. Player 4 comes in for rebounding triangle center position. Player 5 moves to take the right triangle rebound position. Player 4 will fill the triangle point. Player 2 secures the rebound and outlets to player 1. Player 2 hustles to get to the center lane. Player 4 could have taken center lane until player 2 can get there. If the offensive board pressure is tough, players 4 and 5 can stay near the rebound triangle longer.

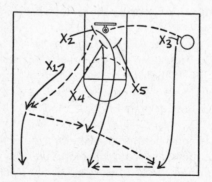

Diagram 3-6

Diagram 3-7 shows rebounder X4 and X5 caught away from the regular rebound positions as the shot goes up. X5 is guarding the jump shooter. You do not want X5 or X4 in the frontal three attack, so X5 will not run the fly pattern. X1 is caught underneath the basket on the weak side. X1 cannot leave or his man rebounds and scores. As quickly as X1 clears the outlet pass, he races up floor. He sees X2 and X3 already in their lanes so he takes the vacant lane. X1 could have blasted out instead of outlet passed.

These two examples serve to show you how to stay with your basic break, despite having two rebounders you always want near the defensive basket. X4 and X5 are rebounders; X1, X2, and X3 are the players you want in your frontal attack.

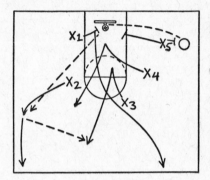

Diagram 3-7

Basic Rebounding and Movement Principles

The two outside, or deep, rebounders are stationed behind the rebound triangle and on each side near the free-throw line. They are almost shaking hands. They are responsible for all rebounds that come out over the top of the rebound triangle. The deep rebounders should be alert for tip-outs (see next section). They should gamble if fumbles occur. They must eliminate an opponent's opportunities to get the long rebound. The deep rebounders should read and anticipate the rebound in order to gain a quick, long outlet position. They must read the rebound correctly, or they will watch the opponent get an easy second shot.

The deep rebounders should always have an 'if' mind for the long rebound or the tip-out that comes into their area. Their mind set should be: "The rebound has my initials on it . . . But 'if'. . . ." They must anticipate and be ready to flash to the outlet pass positions if the triangle has better than a 50 percent chance to capture the ball. The deep re-

bounders and the triangle rebounders must be alert at all times to coordinate the outlet pass as the ball is captured. Deep rebounders, along
with player 3, should possess super quickness—the best on the team.
Racing to outlet receiving positions will also add to the fast break speed.

Diagram 3-8 shows the basic position of the fast break rebounding
team and their first moves in the basic break. The timing of the breakout
is controlled by the triangle rebounders. This is very important to the
success of the break. Power forward player 4, in Diagram 3-8, takes the
rebound. Player 3 immediately races to the middle lane. As player 4
dumps the outlet pass to player 2, player 2 checks the coverage on player
3. This is his passing judgment. This tells player 2 which option he will
run.

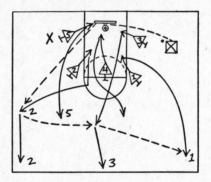

Diagram 3-8

Every rebound will produce a different timing, which makes it
necessary to read and to be on time—not late, nor early. You should
work to have any mistiming occur on the late side, but race to make up
the time. The early break-out sometimes ends up with the center lane
cutter slowing down. This stalls out the break and gives opponents the
opportunity to intercept passes or get ahead of the ball.

Center lane cutter 3 must protect the board first, then break as the
outlet pass starts. If the outlet pass receiver is deep, cutters may cut even
deeper. But the outlet receiver should be sure to look at the rebounder
on the way out to his outlet receiving position. Eye-to-eye contact will
help to nullify any opponent's pressure.

The right-side deep rebounder, player 1, away from the pass-out,
takes one step outside then he breaks down and out. He goes deep,
ready to receive the pass from the center lane cutter, player 3. Or if the
opponents attempt to stop the pass to player 3, player 2 can pass to
player 1 on the fly route. Unless the opponents keep three defenders
back on defense they cannot prevent both the pass to the middle and the
pass to the fly. The defense decides; and player 2 must use his passing

judgment to choose the correct option. If the opponents do keep three defenders back, they give you complete control of the boards. This fear of the fast break has already defeated your opponents. Player 1 should be well beyond the ten-second line as the ball hits the hands of the center lane cutter, player 3. This allows the center lane cutter to see the ball and his downcourt teammate at the same time. Downcourt vision is very important. A common error is the omission of downcourt vision, especially for players who love to put the ball on the floor first.

Diagram 3-9 displays how your team rebounding triangle can be destroyed when playing man-to-man defense. This can happen when your opponents are spreading their attack or when they have excellent outside shooting. As the shot starts up, the defenders box-out then head for their rebounding positions. This expanded offense tries to pull the rebounders away from their team position, allowing the attackers to get around them for the offensive rebound. But the spread attack hurts the offensive team as much as it does the defensive team because the attackers are not in a good rebound position with their big rebounders.

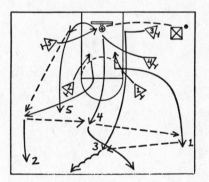

Diagram 3-9

Players 3 and 4 will break to the boards, then fill the center lane cutter rule according to who is the farthest away from a rebound position. If player 4 fills the center lane for the outlet pass, player 3 will take over just as player 4 passes to the deep wing, player 1. Player 3 never stops running. If the defense congregates in the middle lane, player 3 should continue on down court clearing the vital reverse lane for player 4. This act by player 3 will clear the middle lane, as the defense must go with player 3 or allow him the lay-up. If the defense decides to stay anyway to stop the reverse pass to player 4, players 3 and 1 have an easy 2-on-1 advantage from their fly patterns. After receiving the ball in the middle lane, player 4 becomes the fast break trailer. Player 5 checks his opponent, goes to the board, secures the rebound, outlets to 2, then trails the entire break down the court.

Why not try the rebound tip?

Diagram 3-10 demonstrates player 5 getting a hand on the rebound, tipping it out along the baseline, and player 2 chasing down the loose ball. This tip pass is risky; but when the situation on the board has the extreme danger of the opposition getting a tip-in basket, it is the better alternative. The tip pass can be practiced at the same time that you drill the held-ball tips. Your goal is accuracy: Make the tip into an accurate outlet pass. And when you decide to use the tip outlet pass, you must designate an area where the tip will land. This gives your guards an edge in anticipation, in recovery.

The outlet deep receiver goes to the ball near the sideline and captures the tip. The power forward, player 4, cuts to the outlet pass position the instant he sees the tip start. He takes the pass from player 2 to start the break. Either player 1 or player 3 can run the center lane, depending on who clears out first. This can confuse the defense. If player 1 yells: "I've got it!", player 3 cuts to the side lane, going deep, ready for a pass from player 1.

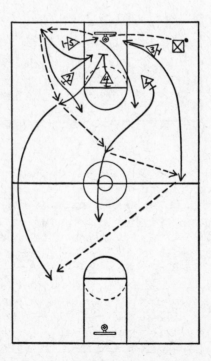

Diagram 3-10

This variation in position changing does not start a real fast break, but it can develop into a fast break up to the ten-second line. By hitting the retreating defense with this delayed fast break, the defense often is caught in the act of retreating to form their key positions. The resulting defensive confusion can result in an easy offensive basket or an unmolested rebound shot. Player 2 follows down the center lane just behind player 1, ready to take over for player 1 if any defense forces him out of the lane. Player 4, on his pass to the center lane cutter, breaks down the left side lane executing player 2's usual lane duties. Player 5 fills behind the break as the safety.

How to get rebound position

There are two major means of running the fast break from man-to-man defensive positioning. You can block out where you are and fill the lanes by numbers, or you can check your man, hustle to your zone rebounding position, then fast break. Both methods have merit, and both will be explained here. We will start by developing the method of going to the rebound positions using the triangular zone board coverage.

Coaches, using the man-to-man defense and variations, have an additional player movement problem to gain the zone team rebound triangle. The opposition against the fast break will magnify this problem by unbalancing their patterns to one side of the floor. These unbalanced patterns, like the passing game, move the key defensive rebounders away from the basket before the shot goes up.

However, most offensive alignments will move only one or two fast break rebounders out of position where they cannot get back to their zone rebound coverages. Three different diagrams (Diagrams 3-11, 3-12, and 3-13) will exhibit a typical offensive pattern requiring the defense to hustle to rebound position as the shot goes up. The only time your defenders cannot hustle to their positions would be when either defender 1 or 2 is caught under the boards guarding his man. But even when this occurs, the attacking guards, knowing the fast break is coming, will usually race out toward their defensive position near midcourt to stop the break. When this occurs, 1 and 2 can release to their outlet receiving positions.

Diagram 3-11 shows a wing attack with the fast-break team defense away from the rebound position as the shot goes up. Diagram 3-12 illustrates the rebound triangle being formed by the defenders hustling to their proper rebound positions. Diagram 3-13 demonstrates the fast break as the rebounders capture the carom from their proper triangular zone rebound positions. Player 3 takes the weakside rebound position and power forward player 4 assumes his center position with player 5 to

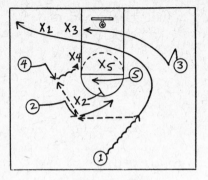

Diagram 3-11

block and clear out the rebound. Player 4 and player 5 work the board like a machine. To be sure of fast break success you must practice using player 3 in the center rebound position and player 4 on the weak side. Also, you might wish to mix player 5 up with players 3 and 4. This would allow maximum versatility as the season progresses and your opponents' team patterns mess up your zone rebounding triangle. By drilling players 3, 4, and 5 at each position, your team would be less confused regardless of your opponent's offensive strategy. Player 3 might be blocked from crossing the key, and player 4 would open to rebound the weak side. This teamwork between players 3, 4, and 5 interchanging rebounding responsibilities and lane changing in the fast break depends upon the skills of those three players.

Diagram 3-11 shows player 3 cutting through the lane into post-up position near the left blocker and player 1 cutting into the corner, impelling X3 and X1 to follow. Player 1 dribbled into the front court and passed to player 2 who passed to player 4. Player 4 shot a jumper. This left X1, X3, and X4 out of their ordinary rebound triangle zone position as the shot went up.

Diagram 3-12 displays X3 sliding across the lane into his normal right corner of the triangular rebounding scheme. X5 slides down to box out player 3. This is the weakness in always going to a normal rebounding triangle. Here X3 could block out 3 and X5 could take the right corner. X4 blocks out player 4 and then crashes his normal area. X1 takes the left outlet lane, and X2 takes the right outlet lane.

Diagram 3-13 shows the basic break from these distorted rebound positions. Players 1 and 2 have exchanged sides, but the others (players 3, 4, and 5) still fulfill their duties of the basic fast break.

The second method of triangular zone rebounding is far superior to the first. Because of the passing game offenses, when playing man-to-man defense, your rebounders may be at defensive guard positions and your defensive guards may be at defensive center. So if you wish to fill the rebound triangle every time, and some teams do, you merely

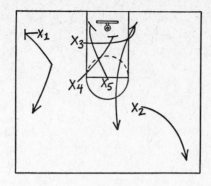

Diagram 3-12

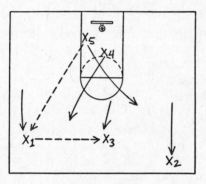

Diagram 3-13

require the nearest defender to each of the vertices of the triangle to block his man out and then go to the triangular zone rebound area. From there you can run either the numbered break, or, if versatile enough, the fast break from these new positions.

The safest way to rebound and then fast break from man-to-man defense is to adopt lane-filling rules. The rules you make should correspond to the lane filling requirements of your triangular zone rebounding. Modifications can be made to allow for versatility.

Players 1 and 2 will always receive the outlet pass and run the two outside lines. They can release with the knowledge that the players they defend must hurry back to stop the fast break.

Players 3, 4, and 5 must always block their own men off the boards, then commence their fast break responsibilities. The men players 3, 4, and 5 defend against will, in all likelihood, be the opponent's offensive rebounders. After securing the rebound, player 3 fills the middle lane, player 4 becomes the first trailer, and player 5 acts as the safety. If a basket is made, player 5 always takes the ball out-of-bounds while player 3 races down the center court. Player 4 steps to get open should the defense try to prevent player 3 from receiving the in-bounds pass.

From time to time, to allow for versatility, the break will be modified. When this happens, we will introduce new lane filling rules. Chapter 5 deals with the details of running the basic break by rules.

How to recover defensively when the rebound is lost but the break is underway

Because your players begin to race to their fast break lanes as the shot flies toward the basket, they can be out of defensive position should your opponents recover the rebound. Most opponents, however, will also be racing back to stop your break. But for safety's sake and because you never want to concede a lay-up basket, you need a method of team recovery when you have begun your fast break but you lose the rebound. This method will also work when your outlet pass is stolen.

A most difficult situation arises when the fast break team loses a rebound they should have captured. The instant that the loss is detected, all players yell: "Man!" That means each player finds his assignment and rushes to ballside position. Be sure to cover the inside or under-the-basket opponents first, even if it means switching assignments momentarily.

Diagram 3-14 demonstrates a quick recovery and the putting of pressure on opponents just after you lose the rebound. Player 2 filled the

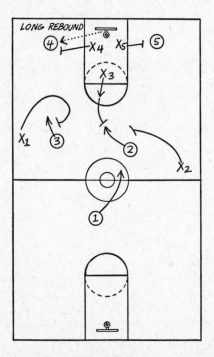

Diagram 3-14

right long rebound position. He had to leave his regular position on the other side of the key. Long rebounder player 1 switched to opponent 3 and player 1 picked up player 3's opponent, until they could exchange. The switching back should take place when opponents are away from the ball or going away from the basket.

One iron-clad rule that should never be broken: Never, *never* leave the man with the ball to make a switchback. Most of the time when long rebounds occur, your opponents are more out of position than you are. The pressure of the fast break requires this defensive distortion.

The Outlet Pass

Some coaches are against all long passes, possibly because the practices did not provide enough opportunity for the passer to become accurate. The quick start of the break will be lost if the outlet receiver is forced to take a pass inside the head of the key, the distance extended from the free-throw line to the sideline. Opponents easily get the third player ahead of the short pass-out.

Early vision is another key to the fast break's success. Time after time a player's first reaction after receiving the ball is to look down to dribble, or gaze at the back court. This is wrong. The outlet pass receiver should develop a quick front-court vision and look for any teammate breaking for the basket.

Work must be done daily on the receiver's moving-pass and catching skills. The outlet receiver should take the pass on the run, yet be ready to shoot the ball over to an open-center-lane-cutting teammate. The outlet pass receiver should develop the skill of indicating to the outlet rebounder that he is faking up, then going deep to eliminate any side pressure. The outlet rebounder would want to use the two-handed overhead pass or the baseball pass to hit the outlet receiver on his fly option.

All drills, including the outlet pass drill, should provide necessary experience for the efficient use of the skill under game conditions. You do not progress very fast unless the drill is used frequently. Consistent use of the drill strengthens the skill until it becomes a strong, successful reactive habit under game pressures.

You should control the defensive pressure in game drills by using less-experienced defenders. You can add more pressure as the fast break players begin to handle the defense consistently.

Time should be monitored for each drill in order to cover your daily practice program. Being specific in skill education requires more drills over the general-scrimmage learning experience.

One big factor in getting maximum skill development comes from the player recognizing how the drill will enhance his ability. He will then attack the problem with greater intensity and concentration.

Superior skill development is based on disciplined drills of the fundamentals, which is a key to successful fast breaking. Individual discipline control is absolutely necessary to maintain skill efficiency through-out the game.

Skill tone and tempo are dependent upon the physical and mental condition of each player. The physical and mental condition of your team will show by the end of the second quarter, the start of the third quarter, and throughout the fourth quarter.

The following diagrams emphasize three-, four-, and five-player drills which your squad will use to get ready for the full fast break with defensive pressures added. The drills will provide more skill practice opportunities in ten minutes than 30 minutes of scrimmaging would do.

The diagrams will give you examples of drilling the details of specific individual areas before combining all the necessary skills for the completely successful break.

Diagram 3-15 illustrates a drill which develops the successful team-ing of the outlet rebounder and the outlet receiver. This is the key to starting the fast break. The rebounder blocks out the opponent and calls the shot as the shot starts to the basket. He rebounds hard, looks on the way down, fakes the pressure, and gets the pass-out to the outlet re-ceiver. Later, add one roaming defensive player to make it a game pres-sure drill. Later, add a player 3 cutting down the middle. Then add the opposite lane cutter and another defender. Now your outlet phase of the break should be reaching game tempo.

Diagram 3-16 shows 2-on-2 rebounding practice with both outlet players cutting down and out for the outlet passes. Rebounders take turns passing out after rebounding. Don't allow outlet receivers to stand and catch the pass-outs. You can use two balls to speed up the rebound drill opportunities by alternating rebounds. The next step would see the triangle rebounder away from the ball, timing his move down the center

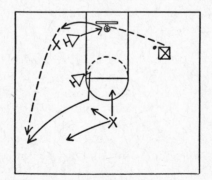

Diagram 3-15

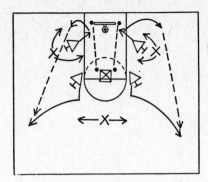

Diagram 3-16

lane as the pass goes to the outlet receiver. Add pressure by placing opposition against the board and harassing the outlet passer-rebounder. This drill merely reinforces the drill shown in Diagram 3-15, but it provides for continuous action which adds to the conditioning of your players.

How an outlet pass ladder helps to teach your fast break

Diagram 3-17 shows the fast break well on its way to the basket. If your triangle rebounders do not have fairly equal skill in running the middle, you must designate the best player to fill the center lane of the break. If the triangle had trouble controlling the board in the early moments of the game, you can move deep rebounder 1 into the triangle, with deep rebounder 2 moving to the center of the floor on top of the key. When you move player 1 into triangle rebounding position, player 2 will become the outlet player to receive the ball on either side of the court, with players 1 and 3 filling the two open lanes. Players 4 and 5 are trailing the breakout, ready to go inside to rebound, post up, or screen.

The triangle rebounder, player 3, who is away from the rebounder, player 5 (who secures the rebound in Diagram 3-17), hustles to the center lane to receive a pass from outlet player 2, as player 4 moves in to capture the inside front rebound position. Player 3 should receive the pass in the middle lane at full controlled speed, and he must be ready to instantly pass the ball to the streaking weakside lane player, 1. Player 1, in turn, passes back to the center lane cutter who has continued his cut. Player 2, after passing to the center lane cutter, races hard to catch up with the ball by the time it arrives at the free-throw line extended.

Diagram 3-17 exhibits a chalk ladder on the left side of the floor, with steps about every 3 or 4 feet. You want to draw the ladder up court

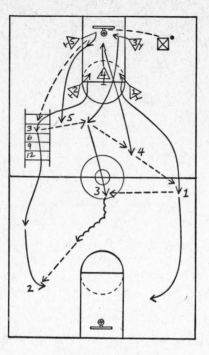

Diagram 3-17

from the top of the key to the ten-second line. The floor-chalked ladder makes outlet player 2 aware of getting down court as deep as possible. The outlet receiver should be aware of possible defensive pressures. But the outlet receiver also must "climb the ladder" as far as he can before he receives the outlet pass. Not only does the rebounder and the receiver have eye-to-eye contact, but there should be a signal (raised fist, for example) which tells the rebounder that the receiver intends to fake back toward the rebounder before going on the fly pattern. This will keep the defensive pressure honest.

The ladder provides the team fast break with many positive results. First, it compels the defensive team to cover the fast break deep, opening up the middle lane. If defensive pressure is applied on the first rung or so of the ladder, the outlet pass receiver runs the fly pattern and the rebounder throws the two-handed overhead outlet pass for the lay-up. Secondly, it demands that the defenders place at least two defenders deep; or they concede a 2-on-1 break (both outlet pass receivers, players 1 and 2). And because player 3 races hard up the middle, most defensive teams place three defenders deep. Thirdly, because of the pressure of the fast break attack, most teams only send two offensive rebounders to the boards. This type of rebounding tactic allows players 4 and 5 to dominate the boards. What in effect has happened is: your team is controlling the tempo and the strategy of the game; your team has taken its opposition out of their game plan, and into your own fast break tempo.

Filling the Lanes

Of the four stages of a spontaneous fast break system, the most difficult to perform accurately and consistently is filling the lanes. Getting the rebound is a definite, pinpointing assignment. It is the player who secures the ball off of the boards. He is easy to see, easy to correct. And it is this man's duty to throw the outlet pass. Again, it is easy to see who is responsible. But who fills what lane depends, among other things, on which option the outlet receiver chooses. Too many alibis can be made. Now add to the lane-filling the fact that different players can start from different positions when the rebound is captured and yet fill the same lane. It is easy to see how complicated lane filling maneuvers can become. Rebounding, outlet passing, and finishing up the break is easy compared to lane filling.

How to interchange rebounding and lane filling responsibilities

The interchange of players filling the rebound positions is very important. Offenses with a lot of motion may put up the shot with the fast break power forward, player 4, or the center, player 5, out away from their normal rebound areas. The nearest three players to the rebound triangle positions should fill the rebound positions as a shot starts. The two rebounders away from the basket should race to the long rebound positions before the shot hits the boards. The skill learning of each position by all players is necessary if you consider this fast-break rebounding option.

When you have this type of versatility your fast break will become awesome. Most players today can handle rebounding and ball handling well enough to use this type of rebounding and these lane filling maneuvers.

Diagram 3-18 illustrates players caught out of regular rebound positions racing to fill new rebound positions. They then fill the lanes that are the nearest to those rebound positions. Player 5 tips the ball toward the sidelines and the open spot. This is the tip outlet pass discussed earlier. The deep rebounder, player 2, hustles to the ball with rebounder 5 filling the left side lane position. Player 5 receives the pass from player 2 and feeds the center lane cutter, player 1, who broke into the right side

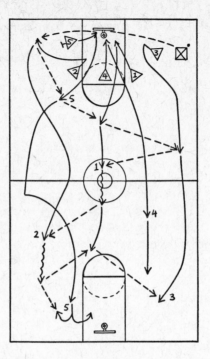

Diagram 3-18

of the rebound triangle initially. Player 4 has moved to the board battling for the rebound. Player 3 is out pressuring the shot. Player 1 sees the tip-out and reacts by racing to fill the center line. Player 3, realizing he was at the deep rebounder's position, hustles to fill the right-side open lane. This corresponds with the rule: whoever guards the jump shooter goes on the fly. Player 4 follows center lane cutter 1. Diagram 3-18 depicts player 5 being outrun by player 2. Player 2 thereby fills the outside lane on the left side. You could use either player 2 or 5 as your safety, requiring the other man to fill the left side lane.

When possible you want the highly specialized positions on the break to be filled by those who have the most skills at those positions. That is why we have player 2 outracing player 5 in Diagram 3-18. Player 2 can handle the perimeter better and player 5 can post up better. You want your players to switch back to their most skilled positions when players are caught doing secondary assignments on the break.

The players are first selected as specialists for the positions of the rebound triangle: the outlet pass receivers, the side lane cutters, and the center lane cutter. You gear your practices to give each player some experience in each of the specialized positions. But you want most of the practice time spent by specialists in their normal respective positions. Your players must realize the fast break will be caught many times in a breakdown move, especially when you are running your man-to-man defense.

Diagrams 3-19, 3-20, and 3-21 are examples of the exchange of assignments that rebounders are forced to execute at times. This could lead to starting in a different lane than the players end in. Exchanges do not occur too often if the two rough aggressive rebounders see their initials on each ball as they take it off of the boards. They accept the full responsibilities of capturing every ball off the board and getting the pass to the outlet receiver.

Diagram 3-19 shows player 1 taking over the weakside rebounding triangular area because player 3 is caught in the corner pressuring the shot. Communication between players 1 and 3 is very important. Player 1 is the general, the center cutter, in this situation. If player 1 can get to the center lane, he yells "I've got it." Player 3 swings to the side lane. But Diagram 3-19 shows player 3 faking back over the center lane after he receives the pass from player 1. A simple dribble to the inside keys player 1 to exchange lanes with player 3. This dribble maneuver always signifies a lane exchange between the dribbler and the lane he takes over. This puts each specialist back in his respective specialized lane.

Diagram 3-20 demonstrates a blastout by player 4. He takes one, two, or three quick dribbles to clear the rebound area and pass to the outlet receiver. Player 3 takes over the center lane cutter's fast break moves, and players 1 and 2 run the outside lanes. Of course, player 1 could have dribbled to the middle, sending the signal to player 3 to race down the right side lane.

Diagram 3-21 illustrates rebounder 5 blasting out, clearing the rebound area with a single dribble, and passing to player 2. If either player 5 or 4 cannot handle a prolonged blastout, you can limit their dribbling maneuvers to one or two. Don't ever let any player do any skill maneuver he is unprepared to do. Player 3 again takes over the center lane cut. When player 3 is forced to rebound or has raced for downcourt fly position, which clears the congested center lane, player 4 will take the center lane to receive the pass from outlet player 2 before passing to deep fly pattern player 1. Player 1 can then hit player 3 in the middle lane and the break continues. Player 1 could dribble to the middle and player 3 would cut to the right lane.

As you can see, the basic break and its options are simple; but the options of even the basic break cannot be stopped by three defenders and two offensive rebounders. As long as you have drilled your players to make the correct choices, the options are too numerous to stop (see Chapter 4). For example, let's let player 4 get a rebound. He can pass to player 1 on the fly, to player 2 in outlet receiving position, to player 3 in the middle lane, or he can blast out. If you sent two men to the boards, the break already has you outnumbered. Communication becomes a key if your players are to consistently make the correct choice.

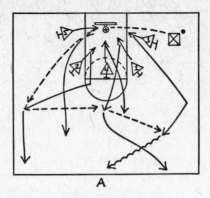

Diagram 3-19

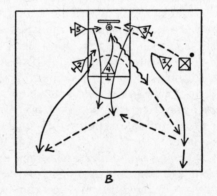

Diagram 3-20

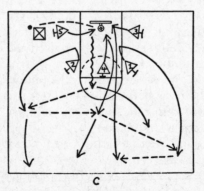

Diagram 3-21

How to get player exchange on the center lane assignments

Players 1, 2, and 4 may take the center lane position. This is considered a secondary option. When player 3 fails to show for the center lane, the closest player will take over. This is automatic lane filling and should eliminate the complete cutoff of the fast break momentum. It can become habitual by drilling the options presented in Chapter 4.

The average high school squad will have two or three good all-around athletes along with two or more who can contribute in more than one position. However, you should always pick a freshman or a sophomore as a backup for player 3. Then you develop him for the seasons to come. This keeps the all-important player 3 position experienced. Players teaching players is an important instructional tool.

You want to keep to a minimum the taking over of the center lane by players 1, 2, and 4. Using players 1 or 2 as the center lane cutter will keep the deep-side-lane cutter away from the outlet pass, the fly pattern. The defense can pile up on the break that uses just half of the floor with the offense, until the open side lane is filled.

Players 1 and 2 may be smaller than your front-line-triangle players. They balance this handicap somewhat by providing speed for the break frontal attack assignments and for long rebounding. Their ball handling should be on or near par with player 3. They are responsible for attacking one side of the court, while player 3 should be able to work both sides equally well.

Player 4 is the power forward who moves in on the rebound, primarily timing and working with player 5 to shut off the opponent's rebounding. Player 4 should be able to rebound from the triangle front point or from the triangle side points. His goal is to give player 3 every opportunity possible to read the rebound. Player 4 quickly races hard to fill the center lane if player 3 moves out or is caught out of position.

Player 4 should be a rebound specialist first, then be alert to fill the center lane in case there is trouble. He generally trails the break and becomes very important in the secondary break. Total individual skill assignments will follow after you have evaluated the personnel you have on hand, unless you can recruit.

Player 5 should be the best rebounder on your squad. He should be motivated to practice outrebounding every league player. That should be his goal.

Players 4 and 5 can be your tallest players or they can be of medium height. But they should have good jumping ability and be quick going up for a rebound. Good faking ahead of passes is needed along with the ability to throw strikes. But they should stay out of the center lane as much as possible. They are your post-up men and your offensive rebounders at the end of the break (the secondary break).

Your defensive assignment of the 3 man is important if you are going to play man-to-man defense. You want player 3 to guard your opponent's shooting forward whenever possible. This shooting forward usually is not expected to be a great rebounder. This puts player 3 out early on the break.

Middle player 3 must be totally unselfish if your fast break is to work. Player 3, with all his skills, can take the ball to the basket, create something, and maybe even score every time. But if you allow this creativeness, your break will deteriorate into a one-man show. The wingmen, players 1 and 2, already tired, will completely stop filling those lanes if player 3 will not get them the ball. You should show your concern by enforcing this rule: on any 3-on-1 situation, wingmen are the only players allowed to shoot. With only one defender, one of the wingmen must be open.

What Can Happen at the End of the Break

Finishing up the primary break with a lay-up is your goal. Sometimes, however, you have to settle for a jump shot with your two big rebounders and the opposite wingmen crashing the offensive boards. Sometimes you don't even get that and you have to enter your secondary break (see Chapter 7).

Diagram 3-22 exhibits a three-player lane fast break with two players back on defense. This is usually what happens—a 3-on-2 situation. The drill starts after a pass has been made to the center lane cutter from the outlet pass receiver—this is the three-lane pattern of the basic break. You can begin by allowing only two defenders in and gradually adding another. You can let the defenders make whatever judgments they wish. You also allow players 1, 2, and 3 to exchange lanes, dribble, handoff, or use any of their options.

Diagram 3-23 shows a four-player fast break with a three-player defense. Now you are fast breaking and beginning to get the trailer into the offense. And you are almost ready to go to the secondary break.

This option shows player 3 passing to player 2, who may attack the strong side or reverse-pass back to player 3. Player 3 then attacks the strong side or weak side. Many secondary phase options will receive treatment in Chapter 7. Diagram 3-23 is presented in this chapter so the reader can see how the four phases of the break can be broken into different parts and taught. These two diagrams can also show you how important offensive fundamentals are; how defensive pressures can be added; and how the strategy can be as simple as two men attacking one, all the way into the full five-man fast break.

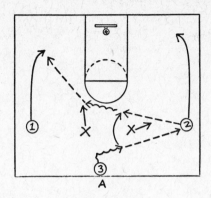

Diagram 3-22

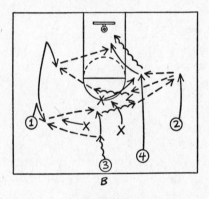

Diagram 3-23

The end of the break usually has player 3 with the ball in the center lane. He can take the ball all the way for a lay-up. He can stop and shoot the jump shot. He can dish the pass off to a wing and stay, ready to reverse the ball if the wingman passes back. He can pass off to a wing and cut to the basket, being alert to get ball side on the defensive player who stopped him. This creates a driving lay-up with a possibility for a 3-point play.

Should player 3 pass to players 1 or 2, some options open for the wingmen. They can shoot. If a wingman shoots it is the responsibility of the opposite wingman to crash the offensive boards. The wingmen can drive, being alert to dish off to player 3 if the defender on 3 tries to help on the drive. Of course, they can drive all the way.

Any maneuver which requires more than these offensive techniques is considered part of the secondary break and will be presented in Chapter 7.

Secrets of Fast Break Communication

This phase of fast break basketball is the hardest skill for the team to learn. But communication on defense, on half-court basketball—in fact, on any phase of basketball—is the most difficult to teach. Kids will talk, talk, talk about almost anything, but they will not communicate on the skills of basketball unless you demand it.

The talking team has a big advantage over the nontalking team. Talking is the glue that holds each player to the group. It makes each player continually aware of what the other players—indeed the team—is doing together. It eliminates confusion and hesitation when countering sudden defensive moves. It will make the options of your fast break system move at breakneck speed, at the tempo you want.

Talking is important in executing fast break variations (not just the options). Talking is important to the team seeking the rebound triangle. Talking is also important to strongside defenders, to players preparing to execute a switch. You must convince your fast break performers of this.

But don't just talk. Make the words have meaning. Work on such calls as "tip," "mine," "got it" when rebounding together, and "I've got the lane," "you take it," "middle," when running the lanes in the fast break. A talking fast break team gives you an added jump on the opposing team. Talking takes the player's mind off of his individual problems, and it makes him a responsible team player. Talking makes you a true fast break team.

Why Each Player Must Learn Each Position

If you taught a shuffle-patterned half-court offense, you would want each player to know each position. The same situation prevails for the fast break. If you use a man-to-man defense, each player must know all the different positions in the fast break because his defensive assignment might place him in a position other than his primary fast break spot, his specialist position. The following six diagrams will show how players can begin the break from unfamiliar positions.

Diagram 3-24 demonstrates the filling of the left side lane by player 5 from the left side of the rebound triangle, as player 4, the power forward, captures the rebound, takes two or three quick dribbles (blasts out) to clear and pass to side-lane player 5. The right corner of the rebound triangle, player 3, blocks out, then fills the left side lane to take over for player 5. You do not want players 4 or 5 in the three-lane frontal attack of the break if another player can fill those lanes. Players 1 and 2 were caught on the same side of the court when the shot was attempted. Player 2 ran the center lane and player 1 started down the right side lane deep. Player 5 passes to center lane cutter 2, who passes to the deep-right-side lane cutter, player 1. Player 5 assumes a safety position, trailing the break, ready to go to the offensive rebound position. Player 4, after passing, trails the break at the right center.

Diagram 3-25 shows a three-player fast break drill that moves from a straight line break into a weave pattern without the dribble. You can use this drill with players interchanging their starting positions. The drill should give each player an opportunity to use the skills of every position, and to respond to quick lane filling. It is also a good passing drill to begin your practice session. The triangle center rebounder power forward, player 4, captures a long rebound and passes to right-side-lane player, 3. The weave starts with player 4 following the pass to player 3, going

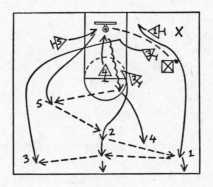

Diagram 3-24

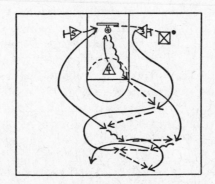

Diagram 3-25

outside player 3, then cutting back in and down court ahead of the ball. Player 5 cuts down the left side lane cutting in ahead of the ball. Player 3 passes to player 5 and cuts over him. Player 5 then passes to player 4 who is cutting in for a pass, and player 4 is ready to pass to the next cutter ahead of the ball.

Diagram 3-26 illustrates the triangle rebound player, 3, defensing the outside shooter and player 1 filling the rebound triangle. Now players 1 and 3 have exchanged positions and duties. Player 1 fills the center lane. Player 5 clears the rebound with a blastout, passing to outlet player 2. Player 3, seeing player 1 filling the center lane, releases and cuts deep to fill the right side lane. This move is executed when your triangle is working the board well. Board pressure troubles could force both players 1 and 2 to go strong on the board before the break starts.

Diagram 3-27 shows an important variation to the start of the break. All five defenders went to the defensive boards because 3, 4, and 5 cannot control the defensive board for you. Player 2, a deep rebounder, grabs the carom and dribbles toward his regular outlet passing receiving lane. Player 2 passes to the power forward, player 4, who has cut down the center lane. Player 4 passes to the deep-right-lane cutter, player 3. Player 1 cuts down the center lane, ball side, to take over for player 4. You do not want 4 or 5 in the center lane if possible. But if player 4 or 5 has the skills to operate in the center lane, player 1 would not have to take it over. This is a coaching decision. Just like different players have varying shooting ranges, so do different players have unlike ball handling skills. Player 5 trails as a safety.

Diagram 3-28 exhibits the basic team rebound positions after the shot starts. A zone defense would have had the players moving in a formation that places them in good rebound position to begin the break. But if you played man-to-man defense, players may be forced out of good rebound position, out of their fast-break starting spots. This calls for interchange of players in rebound positions. It is very important for the fast-break rebounding team to race to rebound positions as the shot goes up. The fast break team must fill the triangle rebound positions first, then they can worry about the fast break lanes.

This drill has the players mill around at the front and side of the basket. Let them move to different positions. All five defensive rebounders must instantly see that the weakside rebound position is filled. They are all responsible for weakside rebounding. The nearest player has the primary responsibility. Player 4 goes to the board and captures the rebound (Diagram 3-28). Player 5 moves in for the rebound. Then player 5 cuts out for the pass-out as he sees player 4 capturing the ball. Player 2 moves to rebound then breaks out to his outlet pass receiving post. Player 5 hits player 2. Player 3 takes the center lane, with player 1 flashing down the right side lane on the fly pattern.

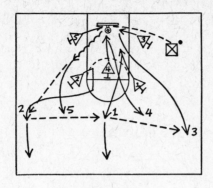

Diagram 3-26

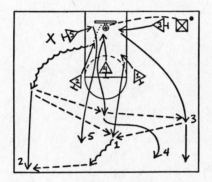

Diagram 3-27

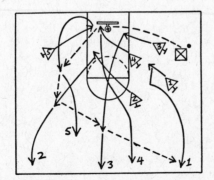

Diagram 3-28

Diagram 3-29 illustrates the offense spread. It also depicts the fast break rebounders spreading while on defense, yet covering the rebound triangle with maximum quickness as the shot goes up. Player 4 takes the rebound at center position with long rebounders flashing out to the outlet receiving positions. The triangle was able to gain regular positions. The long rebounders had to anticipate the rebounder, yet they had to cover the boards and get out to outlet receiving depth to start the break. The remainder of the break is basic.

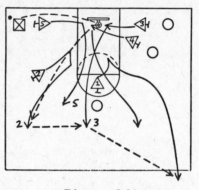

Diagram 3-29

What Must Happen for Your Fast Break to Succeed

To the fan, the fast break may appear as unorganized creativeness, but they appreciate the synchronization of movement and the skills performed at breakneck speed. The coach knows he has to work to achieve this performing beauty. The following points are a brief summary of what must happen for your fast break to succeed. To accomplish this perfect execution, you must emphasize these principles daily:

1. Variation of player movements are essential to open passing lanes. Lane filling options and passing options used with good judgment reduce successes of defensive roadblocks.

2. Fast break speed must be kept within the player's ability to run, pass, and shoot successfully, constantly aiming at an increase in tempo.

3. Organized running lanes and passing options will keep players in positive contact with each other on the break. To run the lanes in a haphazard fashion causes negative results.

4. A quick anticipation to lane filling should be the goal of every player. This insures consistent fast break success.

5. A quick reaction to all kinds of passes requires that the hands be carried waist high.

6. Fast break players must be able to execute the fake-pass away from the passing lane to be used. This skill cuts down on pass deflections and interceptions.

7. Players must recognize and make quick interchange of player lane positions to increase the passing lane openings and maintain fast break tempo.

8. Each different lane option creates several new player responsibilities. So communication is all-important. Talk! On all lane changes call out something like, "I've got it."

9. As an option to the drive-in lay-up, players can make use of the quick under-the-basket, drive-in stops which allow pressure to go by. Your basic shots should show a good shot percentage. Then work on pump fakes, pivot shots, fade shots, and underhand lay-ups, so that your players have continued scoring improvement.

10. Players should have regular success with a shot before using it in a game.

11. Special individual 1-on-1 scoring attempts should cover the dribble drive from the fast break, the jump shot at the free-throw line, the wing fake and dribble drives, the wing jump shots, the cuts into the key, and the posting-up maneuvers.

12. In executing the various cuts and options, the fast break, secondary break, the set-up patterns should flow smoothly from one phase to the other. The backbone of the patterns should be moves to pick up the dribble screens, screens and roll-offs, and setting a pick.

13. These moves can be learned as a 2-on-2, 3-on-3, etc. situation and practiced as such, then added to the overall break according to the player's ability to understand. This system of drill provides many more opportunities to practice a skill than by just scrimmaging.

SECRETS OF TEACHING
THE OPTIONS OF
YOUR BASIC FAST BREAK

4

A ll five players are taught the skills of each position in rebounding and lane filling. During your season many opponents' offensive patterns will distort your rebounding and lane assignments. So if all players know each position and have drilled at each, your opponents cannot control or distort either your rebounding or your lane filling assignments.

Use of the dribble should be held to a minimum, unless the passing lanes are covered; or if you have a great playmaking dribbler, you may want to use him to open the passing lanes. A big key to any fast break is the team's passing ability which constantly looks for and always hits the open teammate, especially the one who is ahead of the ball on its move down court.

The rebounder on the left side of the triangle will take all the rebounds at the start of the learning stages and in our diagrams and explanations. The purpose is to simplify the reading of the break movements. Then you want the rebounder on the right side of the triangle to take all the rebounds. When the rebound goes to the right side of the triangle, you merely reverse the player and ball movements. Then you have the center rebounder take all the rebounds, and the process is repeated.

Secrets to Teaching Player-Floor Relationships

A player who knows where he is on the floor and what to do from those spots is always an asset to his team. You must teach this all-important fast break savvy.

Diagram 4-1 illustrates the total fast-break floor skills organization. The center lane cut can be filled either by a designated player from the triangle, or the best player, 3, can be ordered to take the center lane on all fast breaks. If player 3 is an exceptional dribble penetrator, this may be a good rule. Your options are: player 3 can always fill the center lane; the player at the opposite base vertex of the rebound triangle (forward opposite the rebound) can always fill the center lane; or you can allow the players to read and let players 1, 2, 3, and 4 choose who is to fill the center lane. The first option is too predictable, too easy to roadblock; the second option is too structured; but the third option—oh the third option—cannot be predicted, cannot be structured, cannot be stopped with defensive roadblocks. The third option is to fast break basketball what the motion game is to half-court basketball. It teaches *basketball*.

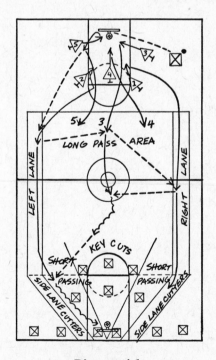

Diagram 4-1

Diagram 4-2 shows the basic fast break. It points out special area moves and passes for player 3. It shows player 3 taking the ball down to the scoring area. Diagram 4-2 divides the fast break into four phases: rebounding, the outlet pass, lane filling, and the finish. Each possible option will be discussed from each phase.

In Diagram 4-2 the left triangle rebounder, player 5, rebounds and throws the outlet pass to player 2. Player 5 then moves down the center of the floor as a safety, ready to move into the offensive board play. Player 4 trails center lane cutter 3. At times player 4 may have to take the center lane pass from player 2, if player 3 is held up or if player 3 has raced down floor to clear the center lane of defenders. Several options for individual player moves will be shown later in this chapter. These options prevent the defense from setting roadblocks in the way of the fast break.

Fast break basketball can be broken down into different phases. Then those phases can be taught separately. You can even create drills for each phase. Those drills can not only teach the fundamentals but also the options that are available in each phase.

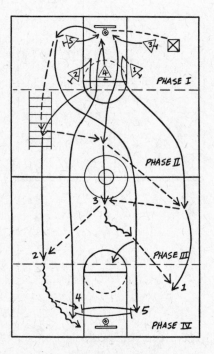

Diagram 4-2

Diagram 4-2 exhibits the complete three-lane fast break basic movements, divided into four phases. It keeps outside lanes wide to force the defense to move a maximum distance to cover the fast break. Defenders who choose to stay in the middle will lose defensive positioning on the wide outside lane cutters.

The fast break is divided into four zones for the purpose of organizing and pointing out the three teaching stages before the final thrust. The fourth phase, the final thrust, leads into the secondary break (see Chapter 7). The chalked-in ladder on the left is to give the outlet receiver a goal to attain depth for the first outlet pass. This deeper outlet pass opens up the middle and facilitates the blast techniques.

The phases on each side of the court are similar, but we will only present one side. To understand the other side, merely reverse the responsibilities.

Diagram 4-1 goes a step farther than needed for the basic fast break. Phase IV is the beginning of the secondary break when your fast break attack fails to gain an initial advantage. Chapter 7 will present all the options of the secondary break.

To use the dribble in a fast break attack, without giving up team ability to hit the open man, is always a problem. Time after time in games you see the dribbler crossing the ten-second line with a teammate open down near the key extended where a sharp side lane pass means a score; but the dribbler continues on, ignoring his open teammate. The dribbler finally passes off where he finally sees the open teammate or when he feels safe, but the receiver now is under heavy defensive pressure.

Thus we have emphasized that the individual dribbler be restricted in his dribbling. A great dribbler knows not to reverse in traffic, is aware of when to throw a pass to a teammate, and rarely ever misses the opportunity for an assist. The poor dribbler is the one who holds onto his dribble too long.

So far we have covered the individual moves of the rebounder, the outlet receiver, the center lane player's cut, and the deep fly pattern down the side away from the rebound. Diagram 4-2 shows the completion of the fast break attack through Phases I, II, III, and IV. By using players numbered 5, 4, and 3 for the rebound triangle, and players 2 and 1 for the deep-side-of-the-key rebounders and the outlet receivers, you will find it easier to read the diagrams. These numbers correspond with the drills and the options already presented.

Phase I consists of the rebounder's options of beginning the fast break. He can throw an outlet pass, or he can blast out. Phase II begins with the reception of the outlet pass, and it ends with the outlet-pass-receiver passing options. Phase III begins and ends with the options from the center lane; Phase IV is the end of the break.

Phases I and II can be discussed together. Player 5, the left-side triangle rebounder, rebounds and fires the outlet pass to the outlet receiver, player 2. Player 2 races down the ladder as deep as possible without allowing the defense to provide interference. Player 1, the right-side deep rebounder, reads the rebound and races deep down the right side lane to force any defense to retreat from the ball. He must be ready to come back for a pass, take it long, or go over the top of a defender who got back on defense. Player 3, the right-side triangle rebounder, blocks out, and he must be ready to cut down the center lane as the pass starts out to the outlet receiver, player 2.

Player 4, after a hard blockout, flashes in to capture the rebound from the front board position. But when player 4 sees his teammate, player 5, capture the ball, he releases ready to run the fast break. Player 4 is the second cutter cutting down the center lane, following two or three steps behind player 3, ready to fill the middle lane if player 3 cuts to the side or if 3 races down the center lane to take the middle defenders with him.

Player 5 comes down back of player 4 to assume a safety valve responsibility. At the secondary phase of the break, player 5 must be ready to rebound missed shots, post up for the pass inside, screen, or execute whatever maneuver you want to begin your secondary break.

The harder you work on Phases I and II, the better the break will become. The above descriptions of the lane filling responsibilities will be followed by all the possible options available to player 5. Player 5 must read the defense to determine which option is best. This is where the success or failure of the break rests: first the correct lanes must be chosen, then the correct option must be made.

A perfect fast break goal can result without the ball being put on the floor. Good defense will try to force the break into a dribble. If defenders are retreating in the passing lanes, the side lane cutters should cut over the top of the defenders (between the defenders and the ball) or change their pace to open the passing lanes to the ball. This points up the importance of versatility in the players' lane running options. But it is better to dribble a few dribbles and then pass, than it would be to hold the ball and wait on the defense to race ahead of your attack. Of course, it is best to pass the ball. No dribbler can dribble down court as fast as the ball can travel by passing. And after all it is the fast break we are after—the faster under control the better.

All the options of player 5 will be presented after we have studied all the possible lane cuts from each phase. Each option is considered based on where the defensive roadblocks occur.

From his Phase II positioning, the outlet receiver, player 2, can pass crosscourt to fly-pattern player 1. This moves the offense immediately into Phase III without hitting the center cutter, player 3. By passing from the strong side to the weak side, the defensive pressure against the ball cannot pile up. The opposition must cover the full length of the court, and they must cover from sideline to sideline. They must always have a defender deep or player 1 will get a lay-up on his fly pattern. This fly pattern is used to keep the defense out of the middle passing lane.

Phases III and IV will be discussed together. This is the final thrust of the attack. It is aimed at going in for a lay-up, or the nonpressured jump shot in the 60-percentage shooting area. Of course all types of options are available on the primary break before you consider the secondary break.

Side lane cutters have a tendency to move in toward the center lane player. Be sure to teach them to stay within 3 feet of the sideline until they reach the free-throw line extended. Such positioning requires the defense move away from the center lane. This allows more room to penetrate the defense with passes. Sometimes the side lane cutter can dribble the ball to the baseline and pass in to the cutters. This is at least a good idea to flatten out the opponents' defense, which in turn allows the receiver of a reverse pass to get a nonpressured 15-foot shot.

The center lane ball handler should weave and fake when coming to the top of the key. This strategy is designed to draw the defense to the dribbler which opens the passing lanes. After the center cutter passes, he must fake his man away then flash toward the ball for a return pass. Or the center can cut hard for the basket. The center cutter should not cut to the basket if the side wing player drives to the basket on the catch. If the center lane cutter drives by the free-throw line, he should drive all the way unless a teammate is wide open under the basket. This rule lets all other cutters know the center lane cutter is going all the way; otherwise, he stops at the free-throw line, passes, then considers his next option.

At the end of Phase IV, just before the secondary break starts, players 4 and 5 cut down to the low post positions. They may receive a pass on the way down to the low post, or they may receive the pass at the low post. If player 4 does not receive a pass, he cuts to the opposite side of the key. Player 5 may cross if player 2 stops his dribble drive. Player 4 could even set a screen for player 5, then roll back to the ball—a good maneuver against either man-to-man or the zone defense (but this is getting into the secondary break).

The three-lane break should come down together with side lane cutters ahead of the ball. This forces the defense to spread and defend all three points of attack. This also opens up the low post options of Phase IV for players 4 and 5.

Phase I. Diagram 4-3 displays typical lane filling positions for Phase I of the fast break attack. Your players must understand and know where these lanes are, when they are to be filled, and by whom. You could rule

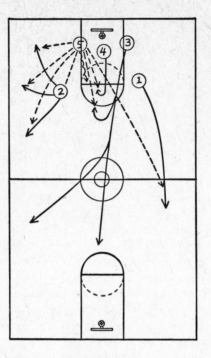

Diagram 4-3

the lane filling responsibilities if you are a structure type coach (see Chapter 5).

Diagram 4-3 shows what happens when the rebound comes off the boards to the left side of the court (player 5). The reverse lane filling responsibilities occur when the rebound comes off the right side. You can determine which to use if the ball comes down the middle rebound slot. Should your personnel dictate changes, you can accomplish those and still stay with the basic break. You merely rule who is to do what. More on that later in this section and in Chapter 5.

Player 5 has several options available during Phase I. First, if he cannot get the rebound, player 5 should tip the ball to the designated tip area (the corner is our favorite). Another area where tipping has proved to be a successful strategy is the elbow area of the key. The tip forces player 2 to run an alternate route. Player 2 goes to the corner, secures the ball, and immediately looks down court to pass to players 3, 1, or 4. Player 3 or player 1 takes the left-hand lane and the other player takes the center lane. Player 4 goes above the key then returns toward player 2 for a pass-out. Player 4 then hits player 3, player 1, or player 2 racing up the floor. Player 2 could, if all the lanes were covered, dribble quickly up the court. An option to this maneuver would have player 3 or player 1 running the middle lane and the other man running the right side lane. Player 4 in this case would move to the left side lane for an outlet pass from player 2.

Diagram 4-4 shows another possibility for lane filling responsibilities on the tip-out play. Player 5 tips wide on the baseline while long rebounder player 2 flashes to capture the tip and pass to the outlet receiver, player 1. Player 4 races up the center lane because he sees it vacant (that is his rule). Player 3 chooses the outside right side lane. Player 1 passes in to center lane cutter 4, who passes immediately to player 3 or back to player 1. Player 2 must race hard to take the place of player 4.

What happens when player 5 secures the rebound instead of using a tip play depends upon the downcourt defensive coverage. Player 5 checks this defensive coverage as he comes down with the carom. His first choice is to outlet pass to player 2 as deep up the court as the defense will allow. This is where the ladder can help you point out to the receiver and the rebounder what option they should use. For example, if outlet receiver 2 and rebounder 5 cannot make the pass to at least the sixth rung, then the receiver (player 2) would fake back to the rebounder and go on the fly pattern. Player 3 or player 1 meanwhile fills the center lane and the other player fills the right side lane. But what if a defensive

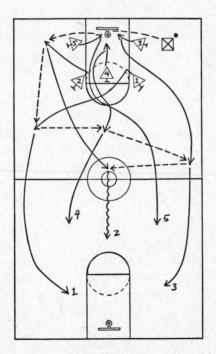

Diagram 4-4

player covers player 2, hoping for an easy interception of the outlet pass. Player 5 fakes the two-handed overhead pass and player 2 steps back down the ladder making the defender think the pass will be on its way. A signal is needed to avoid any possible mistakes—a fist raised by player 2 is the best we have found. If the defender reacts toward the passing lane, player 2 goes on the fly and player 5 pulls the ball back before throwing a leading pass to player 2 for a lay-up. If player 5 deems this option not available, he can possibly pass to player 1 who has run his fly route down the right side lane. Two defenders must be downcourt to stop these fly patterns. Player 5's next option is to find player 3 cutting up the middle lane. A third defender would have to be there or the center lane would be open. If player 3 feels this defensive pressure, he has two options available. He can continue a fly pattern down the center lane (which clears out the defenders in the middle), or he can come back to the head of the key for an outlet pass there. If player 3 chooses the fly pattern, player 4 buttonhooks at the key for the outlet pass from player 5. If all of these options are covered, player 5 can blast out.

But to stop all five options, your opponents would have to move five defenders from their offensive key area back to their defensive basket. This means they would have sent no one to their offensive boards. The result would be an easy win for your team.

As long as player 5 makes the correct choice of options in Phase I, your fast break will be off and running. Whoever receives the first pass from Phase I begins the second set of options known as Phase II. If your break is to continue on down the floor overcoming all defensive roadblocks, the outlet receiver from Phase I must continue making the correct choice.

Phase II. If player 4 received the outlet pass from player 5 or if player 5 blasts out, then the man with the ball should check all three lanes immediately (left side lane, center lane, or the right side lane), for a possible pass ahead (Diagram 4-5). He should dribble a step or two until one of the lanes opens. The runners in those lanes can help by changing pace and even buttonhooking back toward the ball. Downcourt vision is extremely important. You always want your players to pass ahead at the hint of an opening.

Most of your fast breaks will begin, however, with the deep outlet pass on the side of the rebound (player 2 in Diagram 4-5). Player 2 now has many options available. If no defender is deep, a semi-lob to player 1 gets the lay-up. If a defender is deep, player 3 must find the opening. (We have let player 3 fill the middle lane and player 1 the right side lane. This could have been different based on their initial routes out of Phase I.) Player 3 cuts behind a defender who is far over toward the left side lane. Player 3 cuts between the defender stationed in the middle lane and the ball. A third defender would have had to be back or there is no

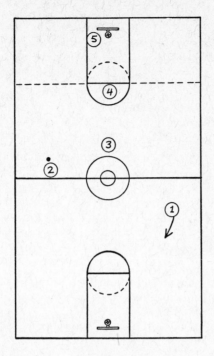

Diagram 4-5

middle lane defender. If player 3 uses the two-sentence strategy above, one lone middle defender cannot prevent him from getting the ball from player 2. If only two defenders were back, they cannot cover the middle lane without granting a 2-on-1 break by players 2 and 1. Even the third defender cannot keep player 2 from passing to player 3 if player 3 makes the correct lane cutting choice. A 3-on-2 break should be the result. Player 3 would want to immediately confuse the defense by passing to player 1 on the right side lane. And now we have entered Phase III.

Should player 2 not see these openings, he still has the option of dribbling. He can dribble, down the left side lane, giving player 3 two lane running options. Player 3 can continue his fly pattern down the middle lane while player 2 advances the ball down the left side lane. This should happen when players 2 and 3 are about even as they race down court. Or player 3, if he is several feet ahead of player 2, should cut to the left side lane and receive the pass from player 2. Players 3 and 1 attack 2-on-1. Player 2 fills the middle lane after passing.

Player 2 could have dribbled to the middle lane immediately. This mandates that player 3 cut to the left side lane. Player 2 hits player 3 or player 1 as quickly as possible, and you are now in Phase III.

Phase III. The ball is on the right or left side lane as the attack enters Phase III (player 1 in Diagram 4-6). At this juncture the fast break usually outnumbers the defense—3-on-2 or 3-on-1. Player 1 wants to get the ball back into the middle as quickly as possible. Player 1 can pass to player 3, or he can dribble the ball to the middle. If player 1 hits player 3, the fast break has an advantage numerically and continues in a straight line. If player 1 dribbles to the middle, player 3 races to the right side lane. This should occur when your players face a 3-on-3 situation. This dribbling exchange of lanes can confuse the defenders, resulting in an easy shot. Of course, player 1 could have continued to dribble down the right side lane until he reaches the baseline. This flattens out the defense and opens up the posting maneuvers of players 4 and 5.

Phase IV. If your team does not have the three-lane fast break, it moves immediately into Phase IV. Phase IV represents your options at the end of the primary break—your secondary break follows immediately with no delay.

Diagram 4-7 shows player 1 receiving the pass from player 3, but player 1 is unable to score. Player 5 races to the block and posts up. Player 4 goes to the opposite block for a rebound should player 1 miss

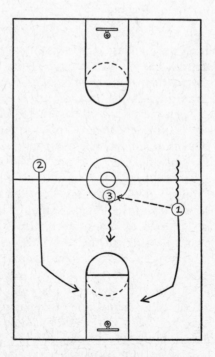

Diagram 4-6

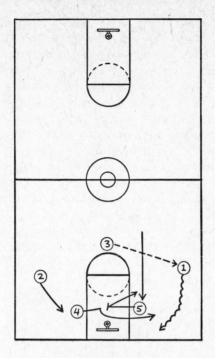

Diagram 4-7

his jumper. Player 2 should also be alert for player 1's shot attempt. If player 5 cannot get a pass from player 1 and player 1 cannot go 1-on-1, player 5 screens for player 4. Player 5 rolls back high. You could even allow player 3 to screen for player 2. You want your secondary phase to place your attacker in spots which will begin your set offense. Phase IV, therefore, depends on what your offensive set attack wishes to accomplish. But your secondary phase also wants to provide scoring opportunities against both the man and zone defenses. Diagram 4-7 does provide ample scoring opportunities inside should the primary break fail, and it does align the players in spots from which you can begin Garland Pinholster's famous Wheel Offense (see Chapter 8). It is also proper positioning to begin UCLA's famous high post offense. The passing game can begin from any alignment.

Secrets of Breaking Down the Options

Defensive strategic moves call for variation and option changes. You have already taught option passing and player lane changing to counter any specific defensive roadblock. Some basic break optional examples include the optional deep move by the outlet receiver, the center cutter running deep to eliminate a defender waiting in the center court for a pass from the outlet receiver to the center lane cutter, or the blast out from a rebound when no one seems open down court.

The passing lanes and player route changing lanes are the result of the defense trying to slow down the original basic fast break lane cut. The following diagrams will give you some idea of how the defense moves to take away one option but opens a new one for the fast break. These are the basic options with only one or two defenders. You can advance to more complicated drills with more than one defender.

Diagram 4-8 shows player 5 rebounding, turning while on the way down, and passing to player 2 on a deep pattern. The defender eliminated the direct outlet pass, so player 5 and player 2 communicate the fly pattern for a lay-up.

Diagram 4-9 shows two defenders stopping the outlet pass. One defender stopped the direct outlet pass and the other defender eliminated the fly pattern. Player 5 would use another option. He passes to center cutter 3.

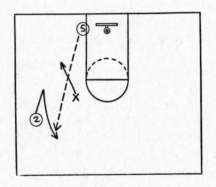

Diagram 4-8

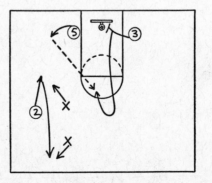

Diagram 4-9

These two diagrams do not exhaust all the options available to player 5. Player 5 could blast out, hit player 1 on the fly pattern in the right side lane (Diagram 4-10), or let player 3 clear the middle and pass out to player 4.

Diagram 4-11 shows the tip-out play to the corner by player 5. This option also can occur when 2 gets a long rebound. Player 5, after tipping out to the corner, fills in the outside lane for a pass from player 2.

Diagram 4-12 displays player 4 using the blastout technique. As player 4 dribbles down court, he can hit either player 1, 2, or 3. The diagram exhibits the long pass to player 1 on his fly pattern.

Diagram 4-13 illustrates some options for player 2, the outlet receiver. The middle has been jammed defensively, cutting off the passing lane to the center cutter, player 3. So player 3 races to the sideline to begin the sideline variation of the fast break. Player 2 can pass to player 3 and cut to the middle; or player 2 could hit player 1 on the fly route. Player 2 would still follow to the middle. Player 2 also has the option of dribbling to the middle. This dribble to the middle would call off the

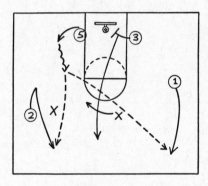

Diagram 4-10

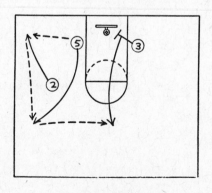

Diagram 4-11

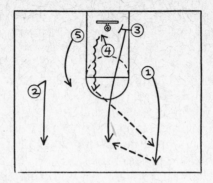

Diagram 4-12

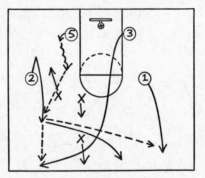

Diagram 4-13

sideline variation, putting the fast break attack back into its basic straight line pattern (for the sideline variation, see Chapter 6). The deep pass to player 1 is an option of the basic break. It is not a variation.

You can use these diagrams to teach drills. These drills would not only teach all the options of the basic break, but also the players would be learning the fundamentals. The most important objective of these drills would be passing judgments.

Secrets of Developing the Two Major Option Areas

Passing drills can also be part of the options of the basic break. By adding defenders as roadblocks, the passer begins to learn passing judgment. We will consider the two major areas where options must be chosen to begin the basic break. Diagram 4-14 shows the first major area, the rebounder's options; and Diagram 4-15 exhibits the second major area, the options of the outlet pass receiver.

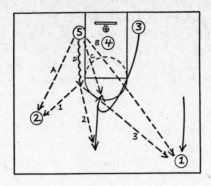

Diagram 4-14

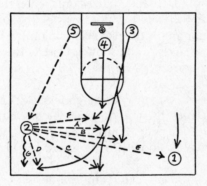

Diagram 4-15

Player 5 rebounds and must choose his option (Diagram 4-14). The defense tells him which to use. Option a is the basic outlet pass to the guard receiver on the side of the court where the rebounder is. Option b is the long pass to the opposite guard and the fly pattern. Option c occurs when player 3 cuts back toward player 5 to provide another outlet area. And option d is the blastout. Once player 5 chooses option d, he creates four more options. Player 5 can continue his dribble, or he can pass to players 2, 3, or 1.

Diagram 4-15 shows player 2 receiving the outlet pass from player 5. Player 2 now has seven options available. Four of those options (a, b, c, and d) are available to player 3. Option a shows player 2 passing to player 3 at the head of the circle. But if player 3's defender tries to cut off the direct pass, player 3 cuts behind his defender. Player 2 hits player 3 on the backdoor. Or player 3 could break by a stationary defender at the head of the key and receive pass option c. This cut must be between the defender and the ball. Or player 3 could break all the way to the sideline and receive pass d. Option e is the long fly pass to player 1 when the middle is congested. Option f displays the pass from player 2 to player 4. This occurs when player 3 has raced down court on the fly pattern, taking the middle defender with him. And option g shows player 2 bringing the ball either down the sideline or to the middle lane by dribbling.

Passing drills can be created all the way down the court. It is important that you drill every player at each position. This is called teaching savvy. Then you set up two or three defenders, after each possible passing and running lane has been run with no defenders. When the defenders are placed on the court, passing judgment comes into play. The more you drill and overcoach, the easier it is for players to execute these options on game night.

Rebounders should use long passes only when their teammates are well out in front of the defense. Such passes should be accurate and semi-looped, just enough for the player to run under. The long pass play is a surprise, used when the defense pulls close to the break's short passing game. The long pass must be practiced daily but it should be used sparingly.

Although passers want to fake defenders away from the intended passing or running lanes, they cannot start the pass either late or early— they must get it there on time. A fast-break passing weakness is having the receiver get a good position with the passer passing after the receiver stops.

Controlled scrimmage can help establish the most important strengths of the passing game. It requires the receiver to meet the pass hard, until the ball is in his hands. The passer needs to lead the receiver. The ball and receiver must still be in motion when they meet. You must eliminate the receiver's error of going for a pass, stopping, and then waiting for the pass to come in.

You must emphasize faking before passing, up-court vision of all five players, choosing the correct option and pass to make, and using a correct pass speed that the receiver can handle.

Once your players have mastered the individual skills, they are ready to begin understanding team skills. But never begin the team skills until you are completely satisfied with individual skills. And once team skills begin they have a priority over individual skills. However, you can from time to time repeat individual skill drills, especially if errors begin to appear.

Secrets of the Long Pass Option

The pressure created by getting the ball to the center lane compels some teams to stack their defense in that lane. When you have an excellent player at the player 3 spot, opponents will try to keep the ball out of his hands. Regardless of why your opponents set roadblocks in the center lane, you can relieve the pressure there by hitting the fly man (the sideline player opposite the outlet pass) for an easy score.

Vision and judgment of rebounder player 5 should be conservative. When player 5, for example, checks his outlet pass area and finds it closed, he turns to check the middle lane. When player 5 sees the middle lane closed, he wants to hit the opposite sideline cutter with a two-handed overhead pass for a lay-up.

Diagram 4-16 illustrates the break variations for player 5. Player 5 hits player 1 on the fly pattern, or player 5 outlets to player 2 who executes a long pass to right-side lane player 1. If the defensive transition against your fast break is slow, these two options may be available all night.

The long pass by player 2 and player 5, the triangle rebounder, is used when the defense is caught in a slow transition or as an option to defensive roadblocks.

Rebounder 5, rebounding clean from the board, has an early look down court, which is the case for all long passes. This early look down court, by every member of the team, is the basis for many fast break

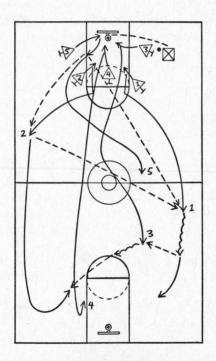

Diagram 4-16

lay-ups. It takes practice to loop and lead the long pass to the receiver. The long pass must allow the receiver to run under it and still maintain body and ball control.

And when the fast break does not produce the lay-up with the long pass, a hustling offense can still gain a numerical advantage. All members of the fast break team should think the lay-up may not be a direct result of the long pass. The fast break members should continue in their lanes all the way till the basket is scored. Many lay-ups are missed and could be tipped back in. Diagram 4-16 also shows player 1 passing back to player 3 after player 1 has received a long pass. Player 3 dribbles to the other side of the court and passes to player 2. Player 2 has the option of the jumper or a pass in to player 4 who has posted up. Frequently your opponents will slow down when they see the long pass. If the fast break players keep running in their lanes, the secondary phase of the fast break will produce a lay-up or an uncontested jump shot.

Secrets of Developing the Fast Break Skills of Player 3

Player 3 reads the rebound, anticipates, and makes a quick decision on the rebound outlet pass. Player 3 flashes down the fast break center lane, while timing the outlet receiver's pass as it comes into the center lane. Running skill is very important here. Player 3 should have versatile moves, not just the direct straight run, in order to maintain a ballside position against any defender's pressure moves.

Player 3 has four options immediately available in his running cuts. He can go on the fly. This should happen when the center lane is congested. It tends to clear the center lane. Player 3 can run a give-and-go with player 2 or he can run a backdoor cut with player 2. He runs the give-and-go or middle cut when the defender in the middle stations himself near a line between the two baskets. This gives player 3 a cut between the defender and the passer, player 2. The defender cannot prevent player 3 from receiving this pass. Player 3 should run the backdoor when the defender tries to overplay the middle lane by exaggerating his defense toward player 2. This backdoor cut is greeted by a semi-lob pass to player 3. Player 3's fourth cut is back toward the rebounder to receive an outlet pass.

If you are running the sideline variation (see Chapter 6), player 3 has a fifth option. He can cut to the sideline to receive a pass from player 2.

Player 3 tries to maintain a maximum but controlled speed. If he slows down, he helps his opponents. They are trying their best to slow down the fast break.

Player 3 should be able to execute the one-count jump stops, the skip-shuffle step, the change of pace, short shuffle dribbles, the fake ahead of passing, and explosive dribble drives to the basket. He should be accurate with the chest pass, the baseball pass from the shoulder, the bounce pass, the overhead pass, and the pass-off to a teammate as he drives toward the basket. Also player 3 should be an excellent jump shooter from the free-throw line. This opens up many an option at the end of the break for himself and his wing teammates.

Player 3 should use the dribble only when all passing lanes are closed, or when the dribble drive is open to the basket without closer teammates. A smart player 3 will open passing lanes to his teammates.

It is best to place the passing lane opening responsibilities on the side-lane fast break cutters instead of player 3. Side lane cutters do not just run the lane and ask for the ball at the end of the break. Player 3 must be dedicated to giving up the ball the instant a passing lane opens to his wing teammates.

Player 3 should have up-court vision of his teammates at all times. He should move fast after passing, to gain an open passing lane for a quick return pass. Player 3 reads the defense ahead of the ball. He changes the fast break options to keep the break momentum. He must know and understand how and where defenses will try to clog up the break.

Player 3 may switch his individual move from the center lane to the side lane; or he can start a dribble weave, if the defense gets an equal number of defenders back against the three-lane frontal attack. The defense calls the signals on most of the break changes. Player 3 must recognize which options are open and respond with the correct answer at game speed. Some options can be called from the bench during time-outs.

Player 3 should learn to recognize overshifted defenses and swing the fast break to the weak side. This gives his teammates ball side positions with passing lanes open, provided the wing players move to maintain this advantage.

Player 3 may attack the strength of the defense if his break has superior skills or if he possesses inordinate skills himself. Player 3 should be able to hit the 17-foot shot and have dribble drive ability along with good pass-off skills, as the dribble lane closes.

Player 3 must be a complete basketball player. Most schools have one freshman or sophomore who is an athlete willing to go all-out to accept the challenge and work toward becoming a player 3. He does not have to have any size requirements. You can make him a small forward or a point guard. You merely have to change your type of defense to accommodate player 3's size.

Players 1, 2, and 4 should have an opportunity to practice player 3's center-lane fast break moves. Outlet players 1 and 2 can start a secondary dribble break with player 3 or 4 filling the open outside lane. Player 3 can even run the fly pattern in the lane opposite the rebound. Players 1,

2, and 4 must be able to comfortably fill in for player 3 occasionally.

This early releasing by the player who is pressuring the outside shot adds another dimension to the basic break. Players 1 and 2 can be your natural guards and player 3 the small forward. Or they can be three natural guards. The early release works especially well against an opponent's pattern that moves their guard defenders toward the corner positions. And if 1 or 2 is the small forward, this early release will destroy your opposition. They will not have enough defenders back to stop your break.

The position of the defensive pressures determines most of the basic break options and variations. A well-trained player 3, however, will recognize what moves will combat those defensive roadblocks. And a skilled player 3 will all but destroy those obstacles.

First you begin with basic drills, drills which teach the one-count stops, the pivots, the direction changes, the change of pace, the shuffle steps and receiving and passing while moving at full speed. All players, regardless of their break position, should begin with these drills. Then you develop the specific skills of player 3.

Outlet pass, blastout, and center cutter drill (Diagram 4-17)

Procedure:

1. X3 and 3 play 1-on-1. When 3 shoots, X3 blocks 3 off of the board. X3 captures the rebound.
2. X3 now makes the decision—blastout or outlet pass.
3. In Diagram 4-17, 3 passes out to player 1. X3 immediately cuts down the center lane for the pass back. When cutting down the center lane, X3 wants to be on the ball side of any defender in the center lane.

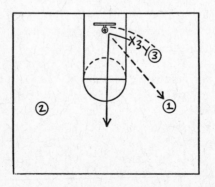

Diagram 4-17

4. If X3 blasts out, he should execute several dribbles before passing to the side lanes. In this case, players 1 and 2 would race down the side lanes.

Objectives:

1. To teach rebounding skills to player 3.
2. To teach blastout techniques to player 3.
3. To teach outlet passing to player 3.
4. To teach player 3 to time his center cut.
5. To teach receiving and passing while running at fast break speed.

Outlet pass and center lane cut without rebounding by player 3 (Diagram 4-18)

Diagram 4-18 illustrates player 5 rebounding and outlet passing, while player 3 reads this and flashes down the center lane to take a pass from the outlet receiver, player 2.

Procedure:

1. X5 secures the rebound and outlet passes to player 2. Player 2 hits player 3 on his middle lane cut.
2. You can place a defender on player X2 to force the rebounder to make a decision whether to pass to player 2 or to the middle cutter, player 3. Player 3 could cut back toward player 5 to receive this outlet pass. Player 2 meanwhile would have faked back toward the rebounder and went on his fly pattern.
3. Player 3 can pass to player 2 or player 3 can dribble.
4. If player 2 had received the outlet pass in a normal position, he could dribble to the middle lane forcing player 3 to take the outside lane.

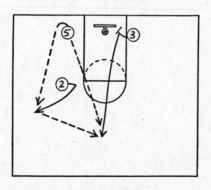

Diagram 4-18

Objectives:

1. To teach either of the rebounders, players 4 or 5, to make the correct outlet passing decision.
2. To teach player 3 to come back for a pass when player 2 is covered perfectly.
3. To teach player 3 to make the baseball pass to player 2 or player 1 on the fly pattern.

Diagrams 4-19 through 4-27 depict the different running routes that player 3 might take. This places responsibility on other players to assume player 3's roles should he not take the center lane. You can add defensive players at certain spots on the floor to impel quick and instant decisions from your fast break players. These routes, made into drills, will teach your attackers to deliver the ball on target, cut to the passes, and take potential defenders away from primary passing lanes. These versatile routes keep that fast break attacking at full speed against all types of defensive schemes.

Diagrams 4-28 and 4-29 show two ways to end the fast break, a secondary phase if you please. Diagram 4-28 discloses a three-man weave pattern. This should be practiced with three attackers against three defenders. Diagram 4-29 shows player 3 passing to player 2. Player 2 dribbles the ball to the elbow. Player 3 dips and cuts off player 2, getting a half-off pass from player 2 for a driving lay-up (more on the secondary break's possible options in Chapter 7).

Diagram 4-19 depicts the basic running route of player 3 in the basic fast break pattern. Player 5 outlet passes to player 2, who hits player 3 cutting down the middle lane. This option occurs more than any other.

Diagram 4-20 illustrates the route player 3 would run if player 5 cannot hit the outlet pass receiver. Player 3 now can dribble or pass to players 1 or 2 on their fly patterns.

Diagram 4-21 displays player 3's move to get open on any defender stationed in the center lane. Player 5 outlet passes to player 2, who passes to player 3 either on the backdoor or the middle (give-and-go) cut. Player 3 reads where the defender is before making his cut. If a defender is stationed too far over toward player 2, player 3 cuts backdoor. If the defender is stationed near the line between the two baskets, player 3 would use the middle cut. If player 3 cannot get this pass, he continues on down the floor clearing out the middle lane. Player 4 could fill this lane; or player 2 could dribble to the middle lane. Player 3 could run a fly pattern or he could cut to the left side lane. Player 3 must cut to the left side lane if player 2 decides to dribble to the middle lane.

Diagram 4-22 shows players 2 and 3 racing down the floor on a 2-on-1 break after getting the ball to the center lane.

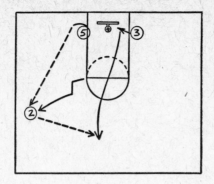

Diagram 4-19

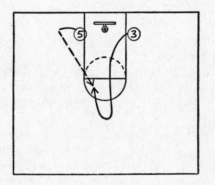

Diagram 4-20

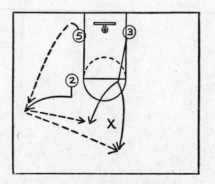

Diagram 4-21

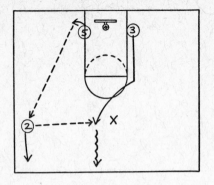

Diagram 4-22

Diagram 4-23 shows player 2 cutting off of player 3 for a hand-off pass near the completion of the primary break. They would begin this maneuver when they see that player 3 is going to be stopped by a good defensive move, or when a 2-on-2 situation arises. This mandates that player 3 move to the left side lane.

Diagram 4-24 depicts player 3 running the right outside lane. This happens when he sees that player 1 has taken over the center lane. This also occurs when player 3 guarded an outside jump shot and takes off on his fly pattern.

Diagram 4-25 illustrates player 3, unable to receive the pass in the center lane, clearing the area for player 4. Player 2 could have continued the basic fast break by hitting player 4 in the middle lane or player 2 could have dribbled there. However, Diagram 4-25 shows the sideline variation to the basic break (see Chapter 6).

Diagram 4-26 shows player 1 running the sideline fast break variation and player 3 coming on up the middle lane. This is included here

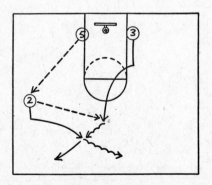

Diagram 4-23

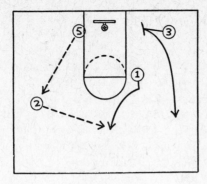

Diagram 4-24

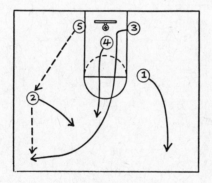

Diagram 4-25

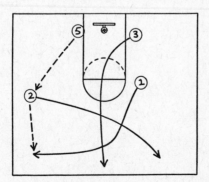

Diagram 4-26

only because players 3 and 1 might fail to communicate the proper lanes. By predrilling and discussing it with the players, an error can become a strength.

Diagram 4-27 displays the dribble into the middle lane by player 2. This dribble takeover of the middle lane forces player 3 to take the lane vacated by player 2. (See also Diagrams 4-28 and 4-29.)

You begin your preseason drilling by running each team 16 trips up the floor and back without stopping, at a controlled speed, and without missing a lay-up or throwing a bad pass. Now your players should know the basic break. Then you add the optional running lanes. Floor defensive pressure comes last.

The fast break can be simplified to make use of the inexperienced players. You can choose how many different lane routes you think this year's team can learn to execute well. You should also study your personnel so you can determine which routes can best be handled by this year's unique players' skills.

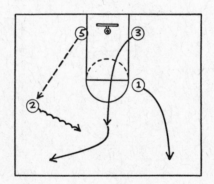

Diagram 4-27

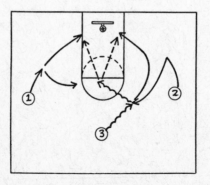

Diagram 4-28

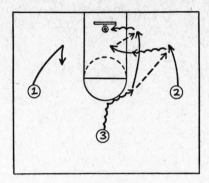

Diagram 4-29

Secrets of Using the Option to Counter Defensive Pressure Points

Diagram 4-30 illustrates the six specific positions of defensive pressures. The number-one defensive position is the offensive boards. It is here that many teams try to keep the fast break from beginning. Some offensive patterns attempt to pull the top fast break rebounders away from the basket. Other patterns will place two rebounders on each fast break rebounder. This is done to try to tie up the hands and the ball at the capture point. Their goal is to force the rebounder to dribble before he passes. Pressure point number one may take away the real quick outlet pass.

The fast break counters pressure point number one with the center lane cutter flashing down deep as player 4 takes the center lane break. This fast break strategy puts two fast break players deep, so that the outlet passer can throw a two-handed overhead release pass for a lay-up. It also provides the rebounder with two short outlet pass receivers, players 2 and 4, most of the time: player 2 on the sideline side of the rebound and player 4 taking player 3's place in the center lane. Defensive teams that try to double-team the rebounder hoping the rebounder will blast out on a dribble cannot cover all four lanes down court. The fast break team will certainly get many 4-on-3 and 3-on-2 situations. This option of the basic break will take the heat off of the rebounder after two or three easy baskets have been recorded.

The fast break offense should have the confidence and will to take the ball to the basket or get the nonpressured short jump shot at 8 to 10 feet. Teams that have set patterns with motion hope to get the rebounds when missed. If the fast break team follows the basic break, its offensive rebounders are in perfect position to secure any missed shot off the fast break.

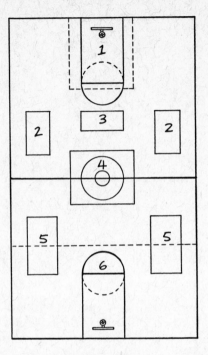

Diagram 4-30

Diagram 4-30 also shows the position of defensive pressure point number two: This defensive pressure point is set to stop the outlet pass. The opposition will slide a defensive player into the outlet receiving areas to attempt to delay the pass-out, or to intercept it, if the rebounder throws the mechanical pass.

The outlet player and the break rebounder work together to develop pass fakes. The outlet receiver fakes the defender by moving back toward the rebounder before flashing to an open area to receive the outlet pass. If covered tightly when flashing back toward the rebounder, the outlet receiver can go on the fly pattern. Eye-to-eye contact is necessary to develop signals. The signal must be well-understood by both the outlet receiver and the outlet passer-rebounder. The center lane cutter can become the second outlet receiver by buttonhooking back toward the pass after his initial cut down the center lane. The guard opposite the rebounder has already gone on the fly pattern. To cover these outlet passes, the defensive team must station three defenders back to stop the outlet pass. Player 3 could run a fly pattern, leaving the center lane open to player 4. Now the defenders must have four players in the outlet lanes. Player 5, the rebounder, also has the blastout available.

The tip-out strategy of the basic break works equally well against both of the first two pressure points. By tipping out, the fast break team immediately clears defensive pressure on the boards; in addition, it already has the ball in the hands of the outlet receiving guard.

Diagram 4-30 reveals that the third defensive pressure point is the head of the key area. This defender will pressure the outlet receiving areas and he will defend the passing lane into the center lane cutter. Sometimes he stands still, then dives into the potential open passing lane. He will pick up the cutter and try to go ballside to make the outlet passer hold the ball. His sole design is to take away the break tempo, allowing two or three of his teammates to get back ahead of the ball.

The offensive player who cuts into the center lane must try first to get ballside of the defender. If this fails, the attacker wants to cut hard backdoor, giving a signal to the outlet receiver. Both of these cuts should carry the center cutter, most likely player 3, deep. This clears defensive area 3. Player 4 meanwhile has moved into this spot, receives the pass, and the break continues. Of course the outlet receiver, player 2, can spot the opposite fly guard, player 1, for a semi-lobbed pass and a lay-up. Also, if there is too much congestion in the center lane and another defender prevents the lob pass to the fly pattern player, player 2 can dribble the ball to the middle lane, impelling player 3 to take the side lane.

Diagram 4-30 also shows the fourth position of the defensive pressure which concentrates on slowing down the center lane cutter as he crosses the ten-second line. Sometimes the defense will try to press the dribbler, or pass receiver, with two defenders. Their objective is to force the ball out of the middle and slow down the attack. Then they drop back to the key and defend against the lay-up or jump shot in the 15-foot area. If this action slows down the break, all defenders can possibly get back into front positions. This defensive move could force the center lane cutter out of the middle.

The fast-break counter-option swings the center lane cutter to the side lane. The second center lane cutter, following three or four steps behind, picks up the center lane cutter's responsibilities. This move eliminates the pressure ahead of the ball without a loss of the fast break momentum. It catches the two defenders going in wrong directions as the left-side lane cutter fires a pass back to the new center lane cutter. A defender must cover player 3 as he cuts to the side lane on a dribble and the other defender must stop player 1 near the basket. This opens the center lane for player 2 to receive a pass-back and the 3-on-2 break continues.

A second fast break counter is for player 2 to initially throw the long cross-court pass to player 1 on the fly pattern. Now the ball is on the sideline, with player 3 in the middle lane and player 2 on the left side lane. A 3-on-2 break is on with the ball in the right side lane. The two defenders must cover this as they covered the play above. This tactic opens the center passing lane to player 3. And the 3-on-2 break continues.

Diagram 4-30 also shows the fifth defensive area where pressure is applied to keep the ball on the side of the court, out of the center lane, thereby preventing further penetration toward the baseline. This defensive strategy attempts to cover only half of the court. When the ball is held on the sideline, the defense, away from the ball, can sink to stack the defense under the basket and key. It allows more perimeter pressure to be put on the ball and still stop a drive. The inside defensive overload would pick up the penetrator.

The fast break must not hesitate, but it must drive deep aggressively. The passing must be quick. Never allow the pressure to catch up with the ball. Get the ball to the center lane before arriving at the head of the key. By running the proper lane cuts and keeping them spread, the reverse pass is usually available because the defense must scatter to prevent the lobbed lay-up. The guard with the ball can always dribble to the center lane by faking a drive down the outside, then crossover-dribble to the middle lane.

If the defense is outnumbered, you must go for the lay-up first and the short-jumper second. Smooth transition from the break into the secondary break should compel the defenders to have to play one side of the court honest. By exaggerating their overplay, the weak side usually has an easy jump shot, and if pressure on the jump shot occurs, a chance for a driving lay-up.

You could even drive the lane down the sideline all the way to the baseline. This flattens out their defense, allowing the easy reverse passback to the middle. When you add players 4 and 5 racing to post up low, and this move usually works against flattened defenses, the pressure on the flattened defense is so great they cannot stop the reverse pass without allowing the posting players a shot from the big blocks.

Diagram 4-30 also shows the position of the sixth defensive area: This is the area where the tandem or parallel defense tries to stop the 3-on-2 fast break. The defense tries to stop the break at its conclusion or they try to slow the break down by spreading their two-man defense. They may even try a two-man defensive stunt, hoping to create a turnover.

By always having the three lanes filled, you are assured of a 3-on-2 opportunity. This should get you the shot you desire; and if missed, it should get you the offensive boards. But should the defenders outnumber the offense, a smooth transition into the secondary phase into the half-court set offense should get you the shot you desire. Defensive area 6, which should be the defender's best choice, becomes a poor defensive retreat if your players can convert from primary break into secondary break into set offense. All defenders must get back ahead of the ball or leave a player open for an easy shot. If this strategy is what your opponents like best, who hits the offensive boards for them? It becomes a race to the other end of the floor. You will win this race because your players have been conditioned to run on every break. If one defender is late, an easy shot results. If all get back in time, the smooth flow from primary break to secondary break to set offense gives your players an advantage. Your people know where each will be while the defenders remain confused and can only guess.

Good fast break teams consistently come up with the lay-up or the nonpressured, high-percentage shot. Fast break attacks display tough cutting maneuvers, never slowing down when the break has the advantage. If the break is content to quickly race the ball down court, then set it up; why waste the energy running? Walking it down will get the same results.

Some coaches will use the fast break immediately after their opponent's fast break. Perhaps you have seen a fast break team becoming flustered when it meets up with a similar attack. Generally speaking, the team that has majored in the fast break finds its own defense weak against the break. The lesson to be learned from this is to get plenty of regular practice in stopping the break. Our break wants to score even after your break scores (see Chapter 8).

Your defense must be set where you intend to stop the fast break attack. The fast breaking team should first decide on the number of offensive rebounders it will use in countering the fast break rebounding. If your offensive rebounders are equal to the opponent's rebounding, you should use three players on the board with the fourth at the free-throw line and one deep. If the board battle is questionable, you would hit the boards with your two best offensive rebounders and keep three back. You don't want to be embarrassed by having half of a fast break come right back at you. If the board defenders have all the advantage, you could go with one rebounder and pull four defenders back. If your rebounding is suspect, you never want your opponents to fast break and get an easy score. The fast break is the most powerful weapon in offensive basketball today.

If you are against a deliberate team motion, you would hammer the boards hard with at least three rebounders, probably four. You should always grab every advantage possible and still be solid on the defensive strategies. When you send a player to the offensive board, he must go all-out. A soft rebounder is like playing with four players.

After the boards, where do you want to halt your opponent's fast break? Do you want to stop the outlet pass, or do you want to slow the break down after the outlet pass? Or do you want to retreat to your defensive basket before massing your defensive efforts?

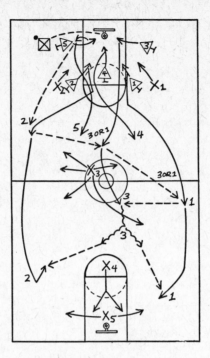

Diagram 4-31

Because you are a disciple of the fast break, you want to know where your opponents will try to stop your fast break. Several days of practice against your opponents' favorite roadblock areas should have your team prepared. After playing several opponents, and facing their varied areas of defensive concentration, your fast break should be approaching perfection, especially if you drilled correctly in its earlier fundamental building stages.

Diagram 4-31 offers a look at a possible defensive strategy of roadblocks. X1 and X2 hit the offensive boards hard. X3 plays the outlet pass or the second pass. X4 and X5 drop to defend against the three-lane lay-up. Offensive rebounders X1 and X2 line up behind each side of the rebound triangle and vigorously go to the offensive boards.

X3 should be placed near the center of the ten-second line, roving to intercept the outlet pass to the sideline receiver or harass the center lane cutter. X4 and X5 are placed in a vertical position ready to halt the final thrust of the primary break. These two players play a tandem defense, one up at the key and the other back under the basket. When X4 moves out to cover the dribbling 3, X5 goes to cover the first pass. When X5 moves out to cover the first pass, X4 drops to the basket area. If player 3 had originally kept his dribble alive, X4 would have stayed with the dribble and X5 would have protected the basket area. This drill forces your fast break players to begin making judgments on all of their options. You can add defenders at each spot to make the judgments even tougher. Instead of five attackers against five defenders, you could get five attackers against several more defenders. Your break, after being overlearned, will have no trouble scoring against seven or more defenders.

Your fast break now has arrived at the full scrimmage stage. Your team has gained the confidence and skills necessary to take the ball all the way down the floor for the lay-up or the short jump shot without pressure. You want to keep the defense limited in the earlier stages so that the individual fast break players will not stray from their organized attack. At first, many young players will break apart at the sign of the first defensive pressure. Have patience.

Many teams call a halt to their break attack and set up in a mechanical half-court pattern at the slightest evidence of defensive pressure. If you have opened your earlier practices with the breakdown drills, your fast break has been overlearned. This overloading technique has ingrained in your players the proper options to use. Heavy defensive pressure will be unable to stop your fast break. If you have also required movement from the basic break to the secondary break to the set offense, your players will not stop the break. They will continue all the way into the set offensive patterns because that is what they have been taught to do.

Once you have established your basic fast break and it moves successfully down the floor against a three-man defense, take the final step by putting five defenders on the floor. Do not turn your fast break defenders loose until you are sure of your players' judgment abilities or they will lose some confidence in the fast break.

Tell your players they are to stay with your basic break until the defense comes up with a defensive problem that will call for a counter, a variation. Once the defense forces the players to use another option, stop them and explain what happened. Soon the team will react correctly to the pressures. This helps the players learn how to make the right move to counter the specific defensive positions. After the players have passed the test on options, you would move to the fast break variations (see Chapter 6).

In time the fast break will begin to develop a definite flow that moves smoothly through the defense. There is a natural tendency for the fast break to slow down if any new defensive strategy shows. The first remedy the team should use is to increase the tempo of their attack; the second solution is to shift to a variation that could take care of the new defensive move. The variations to the basic break can be run from any point in the basic break; but the options presented should be enough to counter any defensive scheme.

You need to work hard. Work to overlearn the fast break attack in order to stand up in all four quarters of the game against all types of defensive roadblocks. Players should develop such confidence that all failures are accepted as player errors, lack of concentration, or loss of tempo to play above the defense. They must be taught never to think failure was due to the fast break concepts or the structure of the fast break.

A Few Examples of the Fast Break at a Scrimmage Pace

You have now developed your fast break completely. The basic pattern and its options are ready for an all-out scrimmage, for a game situation. Your fast break offense puts a shot into the air with two or three players assigned to hit the offensive boards hard. And two players race to their defensive positions, one in the key and the other one deep. The one in the key can help on the offensive boards, and the one deep is purely a safety.

Some opposing coaches believe in stopping and delaying the fast break on the boards. This move is a good answer if they have the re-bound power throughout four quarters. Gaining control of the boards is the real battle for a successful fast break offense. Any delay on the outlet pass allows the opponents to get back ahead of the ball.

When the rebounder feels pressure from both sides as he gains ball possession, he should consider the blastout option. This option leaves two potential defenders behind at the start of the break. Rebounders should be subjected to every pressure possible. Their successful execution and choice of the proper option will make or break your fast break.

The option details consist of two parts: lane filling and choice of dribbling or passing by each individual player. Both passing and lane filling have been covered. We now try to teach a game condition where proper judgments are used. By placing defenders at each juncture, the fast break will be overlearned; now by letting those defenders roam, you will see if the players can pick up what the drills have taught them in a game situation.

Players will learn quickly to execute the right options if they see and feel the pressure shifts. Impress upon the players that the option is not a freelance move but a shift in the offense that the team must recognize. The players must react with a specific optional pass or a lane shift. In the beginning you want to work with one option for a long time before adding another. You might even have to walk through each option whenever one is not recognized during a scrimmage. You would want to show the defensive strategy which would impel your player to choose the second option or the third option.

The next four diagrams (Diagrams 4-32, 4-33, 4-34, and 4-35) are drawn in such a way as to show the passing and lane filling options which might occur in any game situation. They are designed so that you can see how certain changes might occur because of defensive pressure points, yet the fast break proceeds merrily along the way.

Players already understand how the lane running option or the passing option can neutralize specific defensive pressure. They now understand that the defensive move actually calls for the option to be used. The defensive roadblock cries out *use this option*. Each specific option is tied to a regularly used defensive stunt. You are playing a fast-break checker game: the defense sets and the fast break counters.

The next four diagrams illustrate four different variations of the basic break. Each variation should be flexible for some passing changes and organized-player lane filling changes. Your fast break drills should emphasize variables to cover passing-lane and running-lane changes. The experienced team is playing with an anticipated "if" in the back of their minds. These variations are the options at work. They are not different fast breaks. Those will be presented in Chapter 6.

Diagram 4-32 shows the basic fast break option with player 4 cutting down the center lane to receive the pass from the rebounder, player 5. Player 5, in the basic break, would have hit player 2. But the defense has player 2 covered. So player 2 gives the signal to player 5 and races on his fly pattern down the left side lane. Player 5 could hit player 2 on the fly, considered part of the basic break. Player 5 could have used a blastout technique.

But player 5 could also hit player 3 on the center cut. Player 3 was also covered and the area was jammed. Player 3 cleared the area. Player 4 moved to the key for a pass from player 5. Player 4 may pass deep to outlet receiver player 2 when player 4 receives the ball. Player 2 may pass to player 3 who filled the center lane deep. Player 4 may pass to player 1

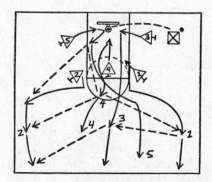

Diagram 4-32

on his fly route, and player 1 passes immediately to player 3. Player 4 would assume the trailer roll ready to take over the center lane, to go hard to the offensive boards if a wing shoots, to cut to the basket ready to receive a pass from the wing, to stop quick to set a screen, or to post-up at a low post position. Player 4 watches the ball at all times and the pass or move of the center lane cutter. The ability to read this play is developed by the multiple drilling of each move. In the beginning, player 4 could have used his dribble as an individual option. Player 1 could have dribbled to the middle instead of passing to player 3. This would compel player 3 to race to the outside right lane.

Diagram 4-33 shows the rebounder, player 5, passing to the center lane cutter, player 1, or to the deep weakside lane cutter, player 3, if the defenders get caught paying too much attention to the middle lane. This acts as a counter to the side-lane outlet pass receiver taking off on his fly pattern because of defensive pressure. This option is called when teams assign a player to cover player 3's cut up the middle of the court. Diagram 4-33 exhibits player 5 passing to player 1 who took over the center cutting lane. Player 1 can pass to either player 2 or player 3. Player 5 could have passed to either player 3 or 2. The dribble option is also open to each player who handles the ball as the fast break races down the floor.

Diagram 4-34 illustrates the center lane cutter, player 3, taking the defense out of the middle. Center lane cutter 3 could have run the fly pattern instead of the sideline pattern. Player 2 has to read player 3's cut and react. This allows player 4, the trailer, to assume the center lane responsibility. Player 2 receives the outlet pass and passes in to the center lane to player 4. Player 5 could have hit player 4 on a buttonhook move back to the ball. Outlet player 2 may pass inside to player 4, who will pass immediately to deep player 1 or to player 3 who moved to the side lane. Player 2 could have dribbled the ball to the middle lane. Player 2 cuts to the center lane after passing, taking over for player 4, receiving the pass from sideline players 1 or 3. Player 4 has a third option of passing to delayed player 5 who can pass to players 3, 2, or 1. When player 4 passes to player 5, he is reversing the action to the weakside. Whenever the pass goes to the sideline to player 3 you could be calling one of the fast break variations (see Chapter 6).

Diagram 4-35 shows side lane player 2 dribbling into the center ready to pass to side lane players 3 or 1. Player 4 can move into the play adding another fast break pressure which overloads the defense. Anytime a side lane player dribbles to the middle lane, it cues the center lane cutter to fill in the side lane vacated by the dribbler.

At every opportunity player 3 should take over the center lane. But there are times when players 1 and 2 might take the center lane over. Even players 4 or 5 have options to take over the center lane. The

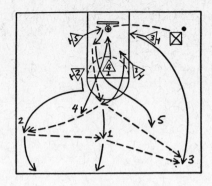

Diagram 4-33

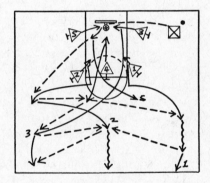

Diagram 4-34

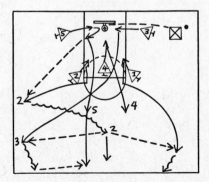

Diagram 4-35

defense will dictate which move you should make. Your players must dominate the defense once they have dictated which move the offense should use. Most of the ball handling should be done by players 1, 2, and 3. Player 3 on the left side lane may get a pass from player 2 and start a dribble back to the middle lane, if you prefer player 3 to always end the break in the middle lane. But this limits the available options, and the defense will stack up against any one option.

Be careful about any dribbling option. Too often players will overuse the dribble options. The ball and the fast break move at a more rapid speed when passing options are used. You must develop special uses for the dribble if you believe that passing should have first priority in the fast break.

Players must be able to distinguish between the fast break basic and the fast break variation. Both have options built in to destroy any defensive roadblock. The fast break variation must be a definite change in the team movement to attack a specific defensive plan. An option off of each is an individual judgment change to take advantage of a sudden defensive roadblock. Your players must always distinguish between an individual option and a team variation. Your basic fast break has enough options for each player that you may not wish to teach a single team variation.

By waiting for the need of a variation to show, you tie the change to a specific defensive plan. The team's growing experience is developing the necessary flexibility to allow them to move swiftly from basic to variation according to the defensive schemes.

While teaching your variations you want to put on only one defensive scheme at a time. Before long you can begin using multiple pressures. Players can react with options to the basic break or options of the variations.

When errors appear, you can go back to the drawing board and design new individual skill developmental drills if the fault is with the individual. If it were a poor choice between basic break or variation, you can develop judgmental drills.

Summary

Your first option problem begins when your player captures the rebound. He can hit either of the three lanes on a short pass or the fly route. And he can always use his blastout technique. You should drill your rebounders daily against two or three players crashing the boards. You then expand by placing defenders in the outlet receiving lanes— first with one lane covered, then two, then all three. Then you combine defensive board play with the outlet receiving pressure.

The second option problem is to eliminate the defensive player stationed at the head of the key. This defender is there to play the outlet receiver's pass into the center lane. By placing a defensive player near the ten-second lane, and by letting him roam to pick off the tele-graphed and mechanical passes, your outlet pass receiver must find a way to get the ball to the center lane. This is the toughest problem. Your passer must bring the fakes before the pass, as well as good judgment, into play. The center lane cutter must run the lane to get the passing lane open and on ballside position. The center lane cutter can cut behind the defender for a backdoor pass. A good fake helps to free the cutter from the defender and may catch the defender going for an interception, taking himself out of the fast break defense.

The third problem is the three-lane move for the lay-up or the short, nonpressured jump shot. You should drill every day against one or more defenders in the key area.

You should now combine all the defensive pressure points. You should drill daily against these pressure points. This will force your players to become optionwise. They will more often than not make the correct judgments; and they can even explain why they made those judgments.

Teach your dribbler to drive hard or your cutter to cut at a fast break speed but not out of control. Try to build on that speed daily in practice. Passers must deliver their passes at the exact moment of the opening.

After your players learn to choose the correct option of the basic break, you are ready to teach the team variations (Chapter 6). Teach only one team variation at a time. And then there will be options to drill for each variation that your players learn.

SECRETS OF RUNNING
THE BASIC BREAK BY RULES

5

Some coaches like to have their players run the same lane each and every time they gain possession of the basketball. These coaches prefer a numbered break. The basic break can also be run by the numbers; but the basic break numbered for lane running can have its options. This puts the basic break one step ahead of the numbered break.

All fast breaks follow this pattern: outlet pass, middle man, second lane man, third lane man, a trailer, and a safety. How you employ these men will determine what type of fast break coach you are.

The middle man is the most important and should be your best athlete. He wants to get the ball to the head of the key as quickly as possible. He dribbles only if there is no teammate ahead of him. But he wants to always pass safely. Whenever he passes ahead and the new receiver dribbles the ball to the middle lane, the middle man fills the lane vacated by the dribbler. The middle man should stop at the head of the key so the ball can be reversed quickly. If the middle man drives beyond the head of the key, he should go all the way for a lay-up. He should have the skills to pass, shoot, or drive from the free-throw line. Shooting should be his last choice. When passing to a wing, the middle man should use fakes away from the passing lane.

The second lane cutter should have run the fly pattern. He can be the player who guarded an outside jump shot, or he can be the guard opposite the side of the rebound. This man should be ahead of the break, ahead of the middle cutter. This guarantees that the three lanes of the frontal attack will arrive at different times, making it very difficult for the defense to defend. The second lane cutter should stay wide to spread the defense, to make the defense cover from sideline to sideline, from baseline to baseline. This man looks first to shoot, then to drive, then to pass back out to the middle man. He must be careful when passing back to the middle man. He may have to dribble back to the middle. If the opposite wing shoots, he should go hard to the offensive boards.

The third lane is usually filled by the outlet pass receiver. He should receive the ball and pass quickly to the middle man. This lane then has to be filled with an all-out sprint. He must always be alert when passing to the middle lane. He may have to dribble to the center lane if there is defensive congestion. If he passes ahead but to the same side lane as he occupies, he must race to the middle lane. His first choice is also to shoot, then drive, then pass when he receives the pass at the wing position in the three-lane frontal attack.

The trailer is used primarily in the secondary break. He will, however, often be open as he moves down the key to take a low post position. He can receive a pass at the high post, at the middle post, or after he has achieved proper post-up position. He should always break hard to the basket for rebound position when either of the front three takes a jump shot. If this man has a good jump shot, you might want to pass to him at high post for the jump shot. When this happens your wingmen should get rebounding position.

The safety is the last player up the court. He defends if there is a turnover against the fast break team. When he sees the three-lane frontal attack approaching proper shooting position, he should go strong to the offensive boards. If no shot results, he is in proper position to begin the secondary phase of the fast break.

General Guidelines for the Team Fast Break

If the outlet player is being pressured as he goes to the side lane to receive a pass, his body positioning should block the opponent from the ball. He should, when pressured, come to the ball to receive the pass. This also sets up his fly pattern. Any contact would result in a foul by the defender. Front and reverse pivoting is a very important skill to defeat defensive pressure. After receiving the outlet pass, he may take a dribble or two to gain the open passing lane to the center cutter. This also gives the center cutter time to read the defender and make the proper cut. The first center cutter, when pressured, can continue on the fly pattern. If the first cutter is covered, then player 4 can fill the center passing lane. The outlet receiver should have medium long passing ability in case he sees the deep opposite side lane cutter open. As a last resort, the outlet pass receiver can dribble straight down court, or he can dribble into the center lane.

1. All players must see the rebound captured. The outlet receivers should be ready for any difficulty on the boards. They must read, then flash to an open passing lane; or they must help gain possession of the rebound before starting the break.

2. Individual skills must be used to check the board pressure, capture the ball, and start the break.

3. The team break is dependent on the outlet pass receiver's judgment. He must fake and execute instantly upon receiving the pass. The outlet passer is the first quarterback, and the outlet receiver is the second quarterback. The quick judgments of these two players really determine the success or failure of your basic break.

4. Run the complete team break to get the knit of the players, then break down to drilling on the parts. Finally, come back to the whole break.

5. The fundamental break skills must be mastered individually before the team can enjoy any success.

6. Use medium pressure until the team is handling the options well. Then you can add the best defense available.

7. Confidence gives the team relaxation and maximum concentration.

8. A chalk ladder on the floor as a teaching tool will show the outlet passer and outlet receiver the area where the pass should hit the outlet receiver. The farthest up the ladder the receiver can go without encountering defensive pressure the better the break will be.

9. Teach all the players to run the center lane well, as the side lane cutters will frequently run the center lane. Add the fourth player going down the center lane when the team is ready. You will have two center lane cutters, one trailing the other by about 15 feet. The second cutter fills when the first cutter has cleared the middle lane because of defensive pressure.

10. Drill the rebounder, outlet pass receiver, and middle lane cutter to develop their timing and get the feel of each position. No two breaks are alike. Each one takes a quick reaction judgment by the outlet rebounder and the outlet receiver.

11. The center lane cutter's timing must be right. Don't allow the defense to catch up and slow the break. Timing should be neither too fast nor too slow, but time the pass by flashing to the lane on time. Remember, the center lane cutter must be able to see the deep teammate as he receives the pass. Passing back to the outlet receiver slows down the break. Passing away from the outlet receiver forces the defense to cover from sideline to sideline.

Teaching the players to execute the specific skills of each position is the basis of the break's success. You can increase the efficiency of the break by giving all five players some practice at each position. But during a game you want the specialist to gain his proper position most of the time.

The rules should be flexible regarding the filling of the lanes. The center lane cutter, player 3 in our drawings, rebounds from the triangle and tries to fill the center lane position most of the time. The rebounder, if it is not player 3, should be ready to trail player 3 in case he vacates the middle lane.

But the deep rebounders, players 1 and 2, should practice from the right baseline position of the triangle; and player 3 should practice from the two-guard position because he will fill those spots occasionally during game situations.

You may want to devise signals for your team to use. This would eliminate confusion by players 1, 2, and 3 but it might also lead to a robotish break. Your variations and options could be signaled from the bench, could be called at the free-throw line during a dead ball, could be changed during a time-out, or you could let the defense always tell your players which option to use.

You may establish rules to govern the play completely. This basic break operates under all these conditions.

You may have players who cannot perform certain skills. Naturally you would not ask them to attempt to do something they were incapable of. You may establish, for example, a rule that your two top rebounders, players 4 and 5, may receive a pass when filling a lane, but they must not dribble. If they do not immediately find a passing lane open, they must hold up the break.

Now let's consider some teaching points for the rebounders, then the outlet pass receivers, then the frontal attack. After that we will discuss the rules and options for each individual player.

General Guidelines for the Rebounders

1. Inside posts should be in constant motion, unless they are posting up. Post-up maneuvers must never last longer than two seconds. Then these players move immediately into the secondary break.
2. The post should start late but be on time to receive the pass.
3. The post should move toward the pass to receive it.
4. The post should fake away before going to the ball.
5. The post should develop the post-up stance. He must develop front-pivots, reverse-pivots, and the drop-step.
6. The post should guard the single dribble with his body from his inside position on the secondary break and also while moving out on the court. The first six guidelines are for the post man at the end of the primary break.

7. The posts should be the best rebounders on both the offensive and defensive boards.

8. The post should have full court vision at all times. After grabbing the defensive rebound, he must quickly throw to the outlet pass receiver, the middle cutter, or the opposite-lane fly pattern cutter.

9. The post should have multiple deliveries to pass to the open teammate as the defenders try to cut off the outlet pass.

10. The post must have quick decision-making abilities.

11. The post should have the ability to blast out if that is called for by the defense.

12. The post should have good peripheral vision.

General Guidelines for the Outlet Pass Receivers

The outlet pass receiver should develop several passing techniques which will give him an opportunity to deliver the ball accurately to the fast-moving center lane cutter or the deep-left side lane cutter. The fast break may have the advantage on the first pass but it can be lost on a slowdown of the second pass delivery. Keep the passes shoulder high. A low pass generally stops the break momentum.

The outlet pass receiver must flash down his sideline lane after receiving the pass and passing inside. He must stay wide and race hard to get back ahead of the ball before it reaches the head of the key. Drilling on these details of the outlet player should have a high priority in your daily lesson plans.

1. The shot is called by the team signaling rebounders 1 and 2 to flash to the free-throw line, backing up the triangle for all rebounds that get away from the triangle.

2. The deep rebounders should close off the key, especially at the front area until they are 60-percent sure that the triangle has the position to capture the rebound.

3. The deep rebounders should be alert to flash to the baseline for any loose ball or any tip-out. If you choose to tip out toward the elbow area, your deep rebounders are already in position.

4. The deep rebounders should fake their opponent with a step or shoulder fake before flashing to their outlet receiving positions.

5. The outlet receiver should jump-turn inside so he can see the pass and the defenders. If he is covered defensively, he signals the outlet rebounder that he intends to run the fly route. He then fakes back toward the rebounder before moving out and down to receive the long lobbed pass over his inside shoulder at fast break tempo.

6. Outlet receivers should always go as deep as possible without running into defensive pressure.

7. Outlet receivers should be ready for the quick, medium-length pass. He can go long as a change of pace if the defense moves out on the medium pass. Give an eye or hand signal to the rebounder.

8. Rebounders control the outlet-receiver move changes.

9. If the inside passing lane is covered, execute a quick single-dribble pivot and pass as the center cutter clears the passing lane pressure. As a last resort dribble to take over the center lane.

10. The fast-break sideline cutters are primarily responsible for keeping the passing lanes open all the way to the basket. They can change the pace, change directions, etc. to open the lanes.

11. The outlet pass receiver opposite the rebounder must be able to run an early fly pattern deep, to force the defense away from the cutter who is to fill the center lane.

12. Players 2 and 1 exchange position skills depending on which side the ball is rebounded. Therefore, both must know the fly pattern and both must be outlet pass receivers.

General Guidelines for the Frontal Attack

The frontal three attackers must have good speed. They are usually players 1, 2, and 3. These three must make good jump shots, have good driving ability, and exhibit good passing moves off of the dribble. If one is much better than the other two, he should always occupy the middle-lane cutter spot.

1. The frontal positions are the quarterbacks at the conclusion of the primary break. They must be able to dribble penetrate and pass penetrate.

2. They should have post-up skills. They can easily slide into post-up position before the defense arrives.

3. They must develop fakes away from their positions before going to their respective frontal attack positions.

4. They must be able to use backdoor moves and fake backdoor before releasing for a pass.

5. They must have exceptional driving ability so they can take some of the pressure off of the lanes.

6. Speed is their biggest asset. Quick starts are essential for fast break success.

7. Medium speed with good moves, fakes, timing, and passing ability will not hamper the fast break.

8. They must have good inside passing ability.

9. They must have good inside passing or they will become a perimeter offense. And if they are to be a perimeter offense, they must have good 1-on-1 basketball ability.

10. The frontal three should have good rebounding ability for deep rebounds defensively and for the offensive rebounding at the end of the break.

11. They must have quick up-court vision.

12. They must have good playmaking ability, or they must be power wings. Use the power wings as a triangle rebounder and move them inside at the end of all the breaks.

13. The power forward, player 4, is trailing the break, ready to go to the board or fill in at one of the frontal positions if he has frontal skills.

14. They must be good dribblers, but they must understand the use of the dribble.

15. These three are responsible for the tempo of the attack.

16. They must show good patience in attacking.

17. These three work together as a team to keep perimeter defensive pressure off of the ball. It is no place for a selfish performer.

18. They should fill the lanes in staggered positions, not parallel.

19. They should be able to move the ball laterally to change passing lanes and drives. They should never hold the ball in any one spot.

20. They should be able to execute good fakes before passing.

21. They should have multiple passing skills.

22. They should be able to penetrate with the dribble then pass off as they drive.

23. They must have an effective 18-foot shot.

24. They must never dribble standing still.

25. They must be able to execute the dribbling hand-off.

26. They should have a quick release and be accurate with their passes.

27. They must be good at faking their defenders then releasing for a pass with good timing.

28. They must be adept at keeping their assignments from dropping inside to help defense the post.

29. They should have the ability to read the rebound and get good fast break position quickly.

Rules Which Govern Each Position's Movement

While the above sections were designed to help you understand what each phase of the break must accomplish, this section will explain the exact movement each player must make. The above sections, if you please, were coaching points. This section is the numbered break. This is where your players would go each and everv time they got possession of the basketball.

The fly runner—player 1

Outlet player 1 is the guard opposite the rebound. He can also be the player who covered an outside jump shooter. Or, if you play man-to-man defense, you could require the number 1 man to always run the fly route.

1. When the ball is shot and the rebound secured on the side opposite player 1, he is to race down the outside lane on the fly pattern. This maneuver frees the outlet passing area.

2. Player 1 should, upon receiving the pass from player 3, pass back to 3 immediately or take the ball to the middle lane on a dribble.

3. If the outside lane break is being run as an option to the basic break, player 1 must race hard to get to the outside lane and receive a pass from player 2 or player 3. After receiving the pass, player 1 must pass again and move to the center lane; or he must take the ball to the center lane with a dribble.

4. Players 2 and 1 must always be alert to player 3 taking over their lane both initially and during the three-lane frontal attack. When this happens, players 1 and 2 must fill in the lane which player 3 originally occupied.

5. Player 1 has the option of dribbling the ball into the center lane if player 3 is covered. When this happens, players 3 and 1 exchange lanes.

The Outlet receiver—player 2

Player 2, in all of our drawings, is the primary outlet receiver. However, if the rebound had occurred on the other side of the floor, player 1 would have been the primary outlet receiver. So players 1 and 2 must each know each other's rules. Players 1 and 2 will frequently exchange positions and duties. But if you wish to simplify the numbered break, you can let player 2 move to the middle of the floor and always receive the outlet pass regardless of which side the rebound comes off on. This means player 1 always runs the fly pattern.

1. Player 2 is to go down the ladder as deeply as possible until he discovers defensive pressure.

2. Where player 2 feels he can receive the outlet pass, he should stop and turn his back to the outside of the playing court. From this positioning, player 2 can see down court as easily as he can see the outlet pass on its way.

3. Should there be a tip-out by the rebounder, player 2 must go into the corner to get it (elbow if that is your choice).

4. Player 2, upon receiving the outlet pass, must check to see if the center cutter, player 3, is open for a pass there. If this option is closed by the defense, player 2 should immediately check to see if player 1 has run his fly pattern and is open. If both of these options are closed, player 2 must make a hurried judgment: Is it better to pass to player 4 in the middle lane or dribble the ball to the middle? This dribble to the middle requires player 3 to take player 2's lane.

5. Player 2, if he is not open on the ladder, has the option of coming back to get the pass or running the fly pattern.

6. If the outside variation is being taught, player 2 must learn to hit player 3 or player 1 in the outside lane and immediately go to the center lane himself.

The center cutter—player 3

This player has to be your best athlete. He has to rebound, fill the center lane, catch the ball on the move, handle it flawlessly, and pass it off in traffic. If you are running the numbered break, you would always want him in the middle lane.

1. Player 3's first responsibility is the right rebound triangle. He must either cover this area or see that it is covered before moving to his next option.

2. Player 3 should, if at all possible, take the center lane. He is the reason why we are running this fast break. It works best when he is in the center lane.

3. If the center lane is covered defensively, player 3 should break back in a buttonhook move toward the outlet rebounder, go on a fly down the center lane (thereby clearing the center lane of defensive pressure), or move to the outside lane.

4. Player 3, if he had so chosen, could have taken one of the outside lanes in the initial stage of the break. This would key either player 1 or 2 to cover the center lane.

5. Player 3 must be ever alert as he, player 1, or player 2 advances the ball down the court. A dribble toward the center lane by either 1 or 2 tells player 3 to take the outside lane held originally by the outside lane dribbler.

The trailer—player 4

The power forward, player 4, is the center of the rebound triangle. Naturally he goes for the rebound from the front of the basket area. He goes either left or right following the outlet pass. He should be your quickest power rebounder. If you are in the numbered break, he would always be your second cutter down the center lane.

1. Player 4 should be a good passer with the ability to take the center lane when player 3 clears the middle lane.

2. He need only be able to run the center lane for the first two passes. He should be able to make one or two dribbles.

3. He will be the trailer who cuts down through the key to set up at the low post at the end of the break. He will be on the side of the ball.

4. He may be hit at the high post for a jump shot. He may be hit at the medium post to start the secondary break.

The safety—player 5

Player 5's fundamentals must be developed to the maximum of his abilities. He is the cornerstone of the fast break. Above and beyond every skill detail, player 5 should feel that he is the initiator of the fast break and be ready to accept this responsibility on each rebound. He will always trail the break until it gets into the secondary phase. He goes to the boards should a wing shoot a jump shot off of the primary break. This positioning not only puts him in perfect offensive rebounding position, but also it places him in the perfect spot to receive a screen from player 4 as the first option of the secondary break.

1. His physical credentials should include rugged power; leaping ability; efficient blockouts; good, strong hands; good vision; and aggressiveness.

2. Player 5 reads the shot well and is always able to see and anticipate when the shot will start.

3. He must block out well yet recover quickly to proper rebounding position in the triangle.

4. Timing is more important than height. Most rebounds are captured below the basket.

5. Player 5 must have good judgment to pass the ball correctly on the outlet pass.

6. Player 5 can add flexibility to the fast break by working on good vertical vision, which would allow him to see the ball and the players under the basket at the same time. It also gives him a quicker advantage to find the correct outlet receiver.

7. He should not dribble out on the blastout unless he is capable of handling this technique. Too many turnovers are made by the big man when he puts the ball down in traffic.

8. He should be able to receive passes in the center lane. He does not have to advance the ball down the center lane.

A drill which will teach the players to read the lane filling requirements and choose the correct one is desperately needed. You begin this drill, first without defenders, then add the defenses, which can teach your players to read the lane cuts. You want to drill all the players who might be filling a frontal lane at each of the three lane filling positions. Players 1, 2, and 3 must be exceptionally solid on lane filling options and maneuvers.

Diagram 5-1 shows a three-lane, straight-line fast break drill, switching to a front line weave after crossing the ten-second line. Diagram 5-1 makes use of players 1, 2, and 4. Player 4 rebounds and passes to player 2. Player 4 races hard to the lane which needs filling—in this case the center lane. Player 4, of course, had all his outlet pass options available to him. Player 2, in the diagram, passes to player 4 in the middle who immediately passes to player 1. Player 2, of course, could have dribbled to the middle, compelling player 4 to fill the left sideline lane. Player 2 could have used any of his other options. The diagram continues with player 1 passing to player 4, who passes to player 2, and player 2 passes back to player 4. Player 4 then dribbles and passes to player 1. Player 4 breaks outside player 1. Player 4 is ready to receive a hand-off pass from player 1; or player 1 can execute a fake pass if he sees the right lane cutter, player 2, cut free over the top of his opponent. The dribbler or

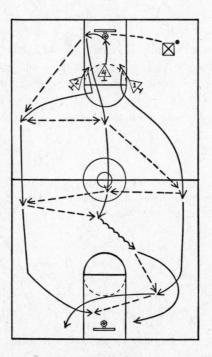

Diagram 5-1

passer executes a quick pass and follows, employing a weave pattern. He goes outside to the basket as the left lane cutter is feeding the right lane cutter, who is driving hard for the basket.

Defenders should be added one at a time. Options are learned and executed along with passing and lane filling techniques, including proper judgment. The attackers do not have to run the weave pattern at the end of the break. They may learn their own secondary break during this drill.

SECRETS OF DEVELOPING
YOUR FAST BREAK VARIATIONS

6

A variation is an entirely different fast break pattern, an entirely different approach. The basic break, which has been presented in the first five chapters, attacks the middle lane with options which will take it down other lanes. The basic break thinks pass then dribble. Two different variations will be presented in this chapter: the sideline fast break and the dribbling fast break. The sideline fast break stresses going down the sidelines, but it will have options to take it down different lanes. And the dribbling break will think dribble then pass. By adding variations to the basic break and the basic break's options, you will have a full fast break system.

When the variations can be substituted at any spot along the path of the basic fast break, you have a very versatile fast break system. Both the sideline fast break and dribbling fast break will interchange with the basic break at almost every juncture.

Let me stress again these two variations to the basic break are not options of the basic break. The sideline fast break attacks down the sideline and not the middle. The dribbling fast break, although safer than the passing break, is much slower.

Use of Variations and Options

The defense tries various moves to blunt the point of the fast break attack. This calls for quick optional changes in order to keep up the fast break momentum. Sometimes the defensive congestion is just so great that a different line of attack must be planned. Enter the variation.

It is very important for your players to understand that the tough basic fast break pattern is the reason why a variation or an option to the basic break is wide open. Mechanical players will say to their coach that they should run that variation all the time.

You will find it more difficult to open passing lanes the longer you run the basic break, unless you have a quick counter-optional move. The basic fast break uses options that force the defenders to think about two or more attack moves at the same time. Because of this optional scheme in the basic break, you may never have to teach a variation. But the variations we present will fit perfectly into your basic fast break system. Your players might even think of these variations as options to the basic break. The number of variations and options that you can successfully use depends upon the squad's basketball fundamentals and their ability to learn and execute different patterns. Of course these variations and options are accumulative. The basic break can begin in your early program. You can add options and variations over the years until your high school team amasses an entire complement for team use. Teach one variation at a time; review one variation at a time.

Variations to the basic break should be an offensive answer to a defensive roadblock of the basic break. Work that variation until the team automatically responds to that particular defensive floor pressure. Then you set another defensive pressure. Lastly, you work with the variation that counters and beats the new roadblock.

Both the basic break and the variations use individual options to gain greater fast break mobility. Your variations also must provide individual options. This freedom within the break discipline should be a move that will counter individual defensive pressures. Options are the offensive answers to individual defensive pressure. An example is a defender denying the outlet pass. Then the offense runs the fly pattern. Variations are the offensive answer to team defensive pressures. A team that stacks its defense in the middle lane should have to face the sideline fast break.

The fast-break team's feel of the offense will advance to a point of anticipation, and reaction beyond a thinking reaction. Lane changes in a specific situation will be automatic. Sometimes you will run a variation just to take the pressure off of the basic pattern.

Secrets of Fast Break Variations

A variation can be as simple as one or two players changing their normal running lanes. Or it can be as complex as switching the break from a center lane straight line break to a sideline break featuring a weave pattern. Most variations lie somewhere between these two extremes.

A slight optional change in a passing lane or in an individual player's cut could be considered a variation. The wise teaching of options should concentrate first on the basic fast break. It should be overlearned and able to stand up under extreme pressure. Add options step by step that will counter the changing defensive situations. Getting your players to go from the mechanical break move to the move that counters individual floor pressures is a tough teaching goal that confronts every fast break coach.

Diagram 6-1 demonstrates a simple, important option where the outlet receiver works with the outlet rebounder to counter individual defensive pressure. But it gives us an opportunity to explain where the basic break options can go immediately to the sideline break. It represents good savvy being used in fast break basketball.

Players 2 and 5 must establish eye-to-eye contact. They need a signal so no mistake will be made. The rebounder, player 5, fakes the pass to player 2 before he throws the long lob pass. This fake by player 5 and the dash back toward the ball by player 2 pulls the individual defender into the original outlet passing lane before player 2 goes deep for the pass over the defense. Your signal between player 2 and player 5 can be any

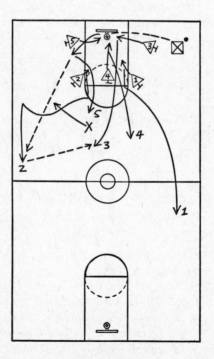

Diagram 6-1

signal you wish. Showing a clenched fist is the best we have found. When player 2 shows player 5 this fist, 2 tells 5 to fake the outlet pass. Player 2 steps back toward player 5. The defense will bring his weight forward. Player 2 then rushes the fly pattern, and player 5 delivers the pass over 2's inside shoulder.

Because player 3's assignment took a jump shot, player 3 should have run the fly pattern of the basic break. In this diagram, however, player 3 blocked out and then went to the boards filling his center lane. Each of these moves has represented an option off of the basic break and not a variation. You could mistakenly call it a variation. Your players will from time to time call options variations. But we prefer to call variations changes in the basic break.

Instead of player 2 passing to player 3 and the three-lane break continuing, lets let player 1 fly down the left side lane instead of his regular fly pattern down the right side lane. Now a pass from player 2 to player 1 would be the sideline fast break. This pattern will be shown in Diagram 6-2. This shows how easy it is to go from the basic break to a sideline break.

Secrets of the Sideline Fast Break Variations

Sometimes a sideline fast break variation will help clear the middle lane for your basic fast break. Sometimes you have personnel which dictates that the sideline fast break would be better for your current squad. Whatever the reason, your club should be taught a sideline variation—even if you choose to call it an option of the basic break.

Diagram 6-2 demonstrates a sideline fast break variation. Some coaches would want to use this break to offset the massing of the defense down the middle of the floor. The break starts as the basic fast break with player 2 executing his outlet move for the first pass. Player 1 races down the center lane across the ten-second line before going to the left side lane. This is a different cut from the basic break. In the basic break, player 1 would have gone on the fly pattern in the lane of his choice (middle lane or right side lane).

Player 1 takes the sideline pass from the outlet receiver, player 2 (Diagram 6-2). Player 3 cuts down the center lane as he did in Diagram 6-1. Player 3 could have cut down the right sideline. Player 4 cuts down the ballside center lane, arriving at low post position just as the dribbling player, 1, reaches the baseline. This flattens out the defense which allows a reverse pass to player 3 or a pass in to player 4 at the low post position. After player 2 passes to player 1, he breaks toward the middle lane. When player 2 sees player 3 in the middle lane, player 2 immediately goes to the right side lane. Players 2 and 3 are expected to adjust their lane assignments.

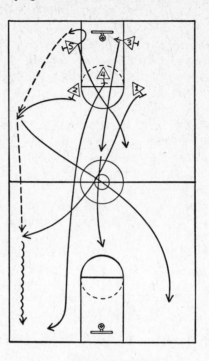

Diagram 6-2

If player 2 could not have hit player 1 on the side lane pattern, then he could have easily passed to player 3 in the middle lane. The reason you have to run the side lane pattern is the defensive congestion in the middle. If the defense places two or three defenders in the middle lane, then the side lane must be open. If there are fewer than two defenders in the middle, they cannot keep you from getting the ball to the center lane cutter.

The side lane passes must be very fast to outrun the opponents who are retreating down the middle. If the defense gets pressure on any of the sideline passes, the motion should go back to the center lane. It is very easy for player 2 to dribble to the middle lane.

Player 4, coming down the lane hard, sets up at the low post for a pass from player 1. Player 5 comes down to rebound the weak side or set up at high or medium post, depending upon what you want from your secondary break.

The low post is usually open when you run your sideline fast break. But if the pass cannot go in to the low post, player 1 should consider reversing the ball to the opposite wing player (player 2 in Diagram 6-2). In the case of the reversal, player 5 might wish to post up low then get into the secondary phase of the break.

The secondary phase of the fast break usually works well when you run the sideline pattern. It is easy to get the ball inside to either player 4 or 5. When this happens all kinds of options appear. Not only do players 4 and 5 have individual inside moves available, but the team can set all types of screens, including the pinch-post move, should either player 4 or 5 receive the ball at medium post.

If the center lane is a major source of defensive concentration, you may opt to use a passing variation to circumvent the congestion before getting the ball back to the middle lane. Diagram 6-3 offers one such solution.

When player 5 rebounds, he considers his basic fast break options. He can pass to player 2 on the outlet pass, or he can hit player 2 on a fly pattern. He can pass to player 1 who has raced down the right sideline. Or he can hit player 4 who filled the middle lane because player 3 has cleared the defense of the middle congestion. If player 4 receives a pass, he immediately passes to either player 1 or 2. When player 3 sees the pass to either 1 or 2, he goes to the corner on that same sideline. The receiver of this pass from player 4 or the long pass from player 5 has a choice to make. This receiver can dribble the ball to the middle lane or he can pass to player 3 in the corner. When player 3 receives the pass, he checks the route of the player who passed to him. This route should be to the middle of the court. This pass would immediately put the offense into a three-lane break. But if this pass is unavailable, player 3 could drive toward the middle of the court. This drive requires the player who passed to player 3 to cut off of player 3 for a dribbling hand-off pass. Now the ball is in the middle and you have your three-lane break. The long passes and player 3's route circumvented the mass congestion of defensive players in the lane where player 3 ordinarily receives the pass.

Diagram 6-3 shows all of the options for player 5. But let us say he passed to player 4. Player 4 immediately hit player 2 on his fly route. Player 3 raced to the corner where player 2 received the pass. Player 2 can dribble to the middle if the defense has not retreated to the middle area. The defense congregated originally at the top of the key where player 4 received the pass from rebounder 5. Player 2 can pass to player 3 if the middle is closed. Player 2 immediately breaks to the center lane. Meanwhile, player 1 has continued his run down the right sideline. Most of the time players 3 and 1 will have a 2-on-1 fast break. If this does not materialize, player 3 could hit player 2 and the three-lane break is on. If player 3 cannot get the pass back in to player 2, player 3 can dribble toward the key. Player 2 breaks off player 3 for a dribbling hand-off. If the dribbling hand-off works, you have the lay-up. If it does not work, your fast break has the ball in the middle of the court and the two wings ready for the three-lane break.

Diagram 6-4 shows a slight variation in the fast break passing and lane routes. Player 3 intended to race and get the sideline fast break

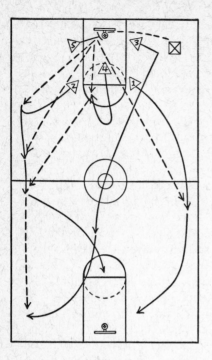

Diagram 6-3

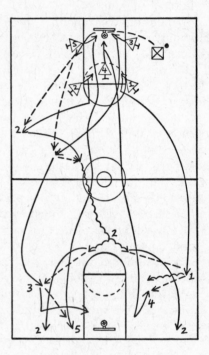

Diagram 6-4

pattern going. But player 2 hit player 3 early on his sideline cut. The break does not slow down or stop. Player 2 cuts behind player 3 as he does on the basic option (see earlier chapters) and on the sideline variation. Either pattern that player 2 thought he was running would have carried him to the center lane. Player 3 hands off to player 2 and the three-lane break continues. In essence player 3 switched the break from the basic phase to the variation. But player 2, upon seeing player 3 clear the congestion, switched the fast break back to the basic break. Neither player 3 nor player 2 had to really know if the sideline break was in order or the basic break was being run.

The beauty of this fast break system is its ability to change lanes almost at will and still stay within the structured framework of your organized breaking system. Players will quickly recognize which break should be run; and your versatile planning allows them to even get their signals crossed and still continue the break.

Secrets of Using the Fast-Break Dribble Variation

Some years you will have that exceptional dribbler. To take away his use of the dribble is poor coaching. Some years you will not have the overall speed to run the basic break and you will feel more comfortable allowing two players to run at fast break speed and a good passing-dribbling player getting the ball to these two "streaks." Whatever the reason, you might want to employ a safer approach to the fast break. Enter the dribbling variation.

Probably the most used dribbling variation is the numbered fast break which came into prominence under Sonny Allen at Old Dominion and later Southern Methodist. Diagram 6-5 depicts a dribble variation of the basic break, using some of Coach Allen's ideas and techniques. Player 2,

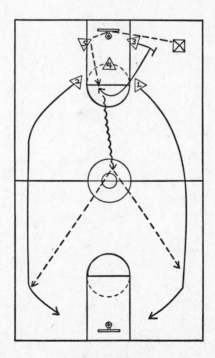

Diagram 6-5

instead of going to the outlet receiving position, takes off on a fly pattern down the left side lane. Player 1 still runs his fly pattern down the right side lane. Player 3 is responsible for getting open for the outlet pass. Player 3 does not have to fill the middle lane. Player 3 is to get open, get the outlet pass, push the ball down the floor by dribbling, and pass to either players 1 or 2 whenever either of them gets open. Whichever of the players who does not get the rebound could be required to race down the middle lane on the fly pattern. In Diagram 6-5, player 5 secured the rebound so player 4 would race down the middle lane. Often this middle-lane running player can get the lay-up because the big offensive rebounders of the opponents would most likely be the last defenders down the floor.

Another variation of the dribbling fast break can be seen in Diagram 6-6. The deep rebounder, player 1, fills the center lane and becomes the dribbler. From his deep right-side rebound position, player 1 executes a quick fake to the weak side, then he breaks hard into the center lane as the pass hits outlet player 2. Receiving the pass from player 2 while running at a controlled speed, he is to continue down court to the head of the key using the dribble. Player 3, seeing player 1 take the center lane, cuts hard to the weak side to fill the vacant side lane.

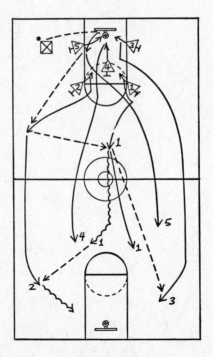

Diagram 6-6

The dribble break gets the second pass up court quicker, but it pays the penalty of not having a player ahead of the ball. The defense can momentarily pressure the dribbler to slow him down. This often allows the defense time to get teammates back to protect the basket area. The dribbler must have excellent up-court vision, and he must be mentally ready to pass the ball to the first open teammate who shows. After passing to either player 2 or 3, player 1 continues on down floor in the middle lane. Player 1 must be ready for a quick pass-back if player 1 can open the passing lane.

The dribbler should have a good move that pulls the defense away from the weak side, then he should pass to the open weakside player, 2. Dribbler 1 must have the ball before he gets to the head of the key in the scoring area. This allows him to fake and set up his sideline cutting teammates.

Diagram 6-7 shows the simplest of all the dribbling variations, which stays basically with the basic break ideas. A pass to center cutter 3 follows the numbered break as well as the basic break. The outlet pass could have gone to player 2, then in to center-lane cutter 3. Player 3 dribbles the length of the floor. He must be able to do this even if there is great defensive pressure. You are running a numbered or dribbling break

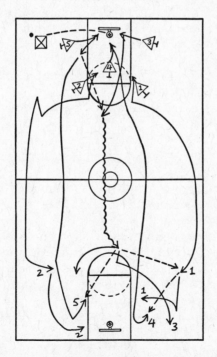

Diagram 6-7

because you have a great dribbler and because it reduces the chances of ballhandling errors. After trying to stop this dribbler a few possessions, the defense will probably try to spread and cover the outside lanes, hoping to slow down the break. This opens the middle of the floor not only for dribbling player 3 but also for the basic break.

The center lane cutter, player 3, recognizes the open center of the floor as does player 5. Player 3 drives down court with a fast dribble. Players 2 and 1 are well ahead of the dribbler, player 3. Player 5 follows and moves down to cover the low post area opposite player 4. In Diagram 6-7, player 3 cuts down the key after he passes to either side lane cutter. Player 4 can time his cut down the lane as can player 5. Player 3 can hit either post man. The left-hand side of the diagram shows player 3 passing to post 5. Player 2 immediately cuts backdoor. On the right side of the diagram, player 3 passed to the sideline cutter, player 1. Player 4 timed his move, hoping for a pass from player 1. Players 1 and 3 split the post after player 1 passed to player 4. Or the offense could have evolved into the secondary phase or into the set half-court offense.

Secrets of a Signal System

When you set up patterns to advance the ball, you are confronted with the problem of setting up a series of simple signals that call for a particular option or a variation change. You do not wish to convey your thoughts to your players via time-outs when you can get the same results with a simple signal. Numbers, colors, pro team nicknames, college teams with similar fast break moves, and numbers can be used to communicate with your team.

First, try to teach the simple moves that will get a player response according to the defensive pressure. Then relate that variation to a name and the players will remember to associate the two. You do not need to give names to the options. Options depend upon players' ability to read defensive pressure points.

Fast break variations generally need to be called at time-outs, half and quarter breaks, and at the free-throw lines. There are times when the defensive schemes are not recognized fully by all team members. So you really need a few moments for the players to recognize why you are calling a variation. Occasionally you will want to run a variation as a change-up. When that situation arises you definitely do not want to waste a time-out. You would want to use your signal system.

A good teaching device is to use the names of outstanding colleges or pro teams which emphasize certain types of fast breaks. For your basic three-lane straight line you could use Whittier. For the side-lane fast break adjustment you could use North Carolina. For your dribbling or numbered break, you could use Old Dominion. A simple voice command would change your variation without a time-out. But a noisy gym will compel the use of visual signals. So a red, white, or blue towel could be used. Players even with signal help must execute the options according to defensive pressure points. You teach the judgment when you coach the optional passes and optional running lanes. The signals will call the variations only.

SECRETS OF DEVELOPING
THE SECONDARY BREAK

7

The smooth transition of the fast break into the secondary break into a patterned half-court set gives this offensive system a continuous thrust on the basket, never allowing the defense time to reset. The basic position of the break pattern as it approaches the head of the key lends itself for expansion to other moves. These other moves are divided into two categories: the secondary break and the half-court set offense.

No one can really tell where your primary break ends and your secondary phase begins. Most will say the primary break ends when you do not outnumber the defense and your attackers must work some attacking move to get the lay-up or easy jump shot. Also it is difficult for anyone to recognize when your secondary break has become your set half-court offense. This chapter will develop the secondary break into several famous half-court offenses so you can easily see how to develop the secondary break into your favorite half-court set.

There are as many secondary phases as there are basketball coaches. To choose the correct secondary phase you must decide on your half-court set against the man-to-man and against the zone. If, for example, you want to run a motion game from a 1-2-2 set, you must make sure the secondary phase of your fast break ends in a 1-2-2 alignment. Several secondary phases are presented to help you make your choice.

Secondary phases must begin where your fast break ends. Although the primary goal of the fast break is to get there first with the most, it will not always happen that way.

Your secondary phase begins when the primary wave fails to gain the superiority of numbers. Your secondary phase must have movement, and it must present several options with opportunities to score. Your set offense follows the failure of the secondary phase. This type of offensive system never allows the defense an opportunity to reset, to rest: the offense continuously attacks the basket.

Sometimes the defense is back in body but not really mentally ready to play team defense. This time span lasts anywhere from a split second to a couple of seconds. A ball club that uses the fast break for a lay-up or quick jump shot on the initial thrust and then resets is not getting the maximum out of their fast break. The fast break club needs continuity at the end of their initial thrust, which prevents the defenders from finding their own man or getting to their zone areas while the offense resets.

The initial thrust of a fast break can come from a turnover, from an outlet pass-and-go situation, or against the slowness of the defense in getting back. The secondary phase experiences success when the defense is caught confused or not alert at the end of the primary break. Trying to place your opponents at a disadvantage is championship basketball.

There are many ways you can describe this period. "Freelance interim period" John McLendon called it. Other coaches want it more structured. It is the coach's choice. But if you want your wingmen to cross underneath the basket, you must work on a rule which prevents them from running into each other. Let the right lane cutter go low and the left lane cutter go above the second lane marker, for example.

Secrets to Developing the First Moves in the Secondary Break

Because it would be a debate as to when the secondary break would begin and the primary break end, we will begin with Phase IV of the primary break (see Chapter 4). We will use players 1, 2, and 3 to describe these moves. Player 2 will occupy the left fast break lane, player 1 the right sideline, and player 3 will be in the middle lane.

Each of the three have an initial chance to drive for the basket; stop and shoot a jump shot; or drive until cut off and then pass off the dribble to an open teammate. That is surely the end of the primary break. But there are moves which are available at the inception of the secondary break even when the attackers outnumber the defenders.

Diagram 7-1 displays the simplest move of them all, the give-and-go. All players have the opportunity to pass to a teammate and then cut between the ball and the defender for a pass and a driving lay-up. Player 3 passes to player 2 and cuts down the lane for a pass back to himself. This tactic gives player 3 a drive to the basket and a possible 3-point play. This move will work even when the offense has the defense at a 3-on-2 stage.

Diagram 7-2 reveals the backdoor play which is also available when the offense outnumbers the defense. Player 3 drives to the head of the key. Player 2 jump-stops, and player 2 fakes a step or two back out toward the elbow for a jump shot. Player 3 aids the fake by motioning a pass to player 2. Player 3 pulls the ball back in while looking at player 2. Player 2, in order not to create a turnover, can give player 3 the fist signal, meaning player 2 is going backdoor. Player 3 delivers the bounce pass for a lay-up. This backdoor play works best when there is defensive pressure put on both players 2 and 3.

Diagram 7-3 shows a continuation out of either of these first two options. It still involves only the frontal three. After player 3 passes to player 2, player 2 drives toward the head of the key. Player 3 times his move so he will break off of player 2 for the hand-off pass and the driving lay-up. Diagram 7-4 shows the same move, except player 3 decided not to pass to player 2 but took the ball to player 2 on the dribble.

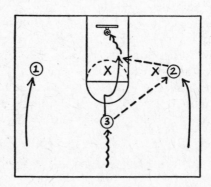

Diagram 7-1

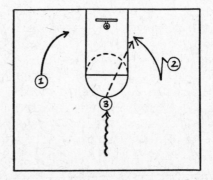

Diagram 7-2

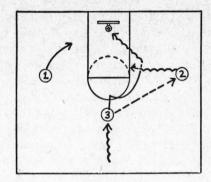

Diagram 7-3

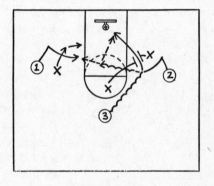

Diagram 7-4

Player 2 comes hard off of player 3 after player 2 has faked the backdoor cut. Player 2 uses player 3 and player 3's defender. Player 2 might have the drive all the way for the score. Player 3 should roll in case there is a defensive switch. If there were one, player 3 could get the inside position on his new defender for a pass from player 2 and a power lay-up. Meanwhile player 1 should be trying to get between his defender and the ball. Because player 1's defender frequently watches the strongside so he can help, player 1 should be able to free himself for this pass and a possible 3-point play.

There are many other three-man plays that can be worked before you invite the trailer and the safety to take part in the secondary break. There are all kinds of screens-and-rolls and weakside picks which would be very effective. You, as coach, must search your philosophy to decide which, if any, of the three-man plays, you want to utilize to end your primary break and start your secondary break.

Diagram 7-5 illustrates all five attackers getting involved in the secondary break. Before explaining Diagram 7-5, you realize you could have passed to player 4 or player 5 at the low post and let them go 1-on-1. You will not believe how effective this simple move is until you have run the break a few years. Usually players 4 and 5 get to the block long before their defenders arrive. This means that big players 4 and 5 are defensed by the small guards who are trying to stop the fast break. Players 4 and 5, if they have been taught to get proper post position and hold it, will frequently have a small guard defender on their back. A pass inside and a drop-step power move usually nets a 3-point play. Your players 4 and 5 have been taught to run all night long. Late in the game the defenders on players 4 and 5 start to slow down. Players 4 and 5, especially if they have their minds set on "attacking, attacking, attacking," will reap great rewards near game's end.

If either player 4 or player 5 have great jump shots, Diagram 7-5 is almost unstoppable. Player 3 has passed to player 2 and he has started to move away from his receiver. This gives player 2 room to operate 1-on-1, and it allows player 3 to try to set up his move back to the ball (Diagrams 7-1, 7-3, and 7-4). It also opens up the elbow area for player 4. Player 4 has an immediate jump shot when player 2 hits him. Meanwhile player 5 has raced to the big block opposite the ball for the weakside rebound. Player 1 is setting up his man so he can receive a reverse pass should player 4 want to reverse the ball. And player 1 is watching to see if he needs to go to the offensive boards if a shot is taken. Players 1 and 5 should control the primary rebound area on any shot taken. If players 2 or 4 decide not to shoot because of defensive pressure, player 5 tries to set up his man for a power move inside. If the defender on player 5 tries to stop the direct pass from player 4 to player 5, the lob from player 4 to player 5 would create a lay-up opportunity. There is no defender behind

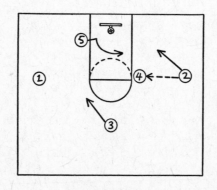

Diagram 7-5

player 5. But if player 5 gets the ball in the key near the basket on a direct pass from player 4, a power lay-up will result, usually a 3-point play. If the defender on player 5 did get enough help to prevent the easy shot, a pass from player 4 to player 1 and a two-man play between player 1 and player 5 should get the lay-up.

Meanwhile players 2 and 3 have set their men up so they can run a crossing pattern over the high-post player, 4 (Diagram 7-6). The player who passed the ball, player 2 in the diagram, should go screen for the other player, player 3. Of course, player 3 could have initially gone to screen player 1 and taken player 1's place. This means that player 1 is coming off of two screens around player 4 for what will be an easy jump shot. This is a simple illustration of how the offense moves from primary break to secondary break to patterned half-court attack.

Players 4 and 5 should go to low post instead of high post if possible. They should post-up for about two seconds while the wing man with the ball tries to get the ball inside at the big block (Diagram 7-7). If after two

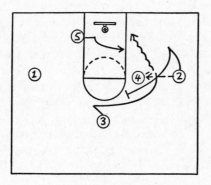

Diagram 7-6

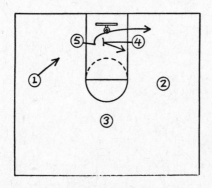

Diagram 7-7

seconds the pass has not come inside, the post man on the side of the ball should go screen for the opposite post player. The screener should roll back to the ball. Player 4, in Diagram 7-7, is the screener; and player 5 accepts the screen. Player 5 should race along the baseline as far as he has to go to receive the ball from player 2. Player 4 should roll back to a semi-high-post spot. Now regardless of the defense, man-to-man or a zone, the options of Diagram 7-8 cannot be stopped.

Let's first consider Diagram 7-8 against the man-to-man defense. Should player 2, the wing with the ball in Diagram 7-7, pass to player 5, player 4 has two options available. Player 4 can allow himself to be used as a back blind pick by player 3. This usually gets player 3 the pass and a power lay-up. Player 5 could wait and allow player 4 to slide back down and post up his defender on the big block. Or player 2 could have passed to player 3 who passes to player 1 at the elbow and runs the pinch-the-post move of the Triple Post Offense.

If the attackers are faced with a zone defense, player 2 could have hit player 4 at a semi-high-post position. Player 5, upon seeing this pass, moves along the baseline for a pass from player 4 and the lay-up. Player 5's rule is to always go opposite if the pass goes to the high post. If player 2 had hit player 5 along the baseline, player 4's rule would have been to roll to low post, just like he would have done against a man-to-man defense. Player 2 could have reversed the ball around the horn to player 3 then to player 1, and begin weakside movement (see the section on Boston College Zone Offense). Or player 2 could skip a pass to player 1 for an easy jump shot. Player 1 has been seeking the hole in the zone defense. This set-up of Diagram 7-8 is the offense made famous by Dr. Tom Davis at Boston College and at Stanford University. It is one of the better zone offenses in basketball today.

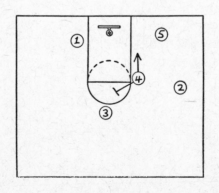

Diagram 7-8

How to Get from the Secondary Break into a Famous Set Offense

There is not enough space for this book to cover getting from the secondary break into all known half-court offenses. So we have decided to consider only a few transition plays. From those few presented, you can see how to go from the secondary offense to the offense you presently use, even if it is not one of the famous offenses. We will present the Go Behind, the Baseline Shuffle, the Wheel Offense, and the UCLA Power Game against the man-to-man defense. Against the zone defenses we will present the Boston College Overload and the Marquette Zone Pattern.

The principles which govern how you will accomplish getting to your favorite mode of half-court are simple. First make sure that whatever you teach in going from the secondary break to the half-court pattern have similar alignments, or you can get to those alignments with a minimum of movement. Second, make sure that you do not rearrange that alignment when you move from the primary break to the secondary break.

Moving from the fast break drive to a designated pattern offense should be simple and smooth. The pattern starts from the fast-break players' positions. If the pattern is a continuous move, the offensive pressure is still on the defense. Your fast break may have caused the defensive players to pick up offensive players other than their original assignments. This offensive pressure can create mismatches. The defense may catch up with the break and still be in a transitional period. The fast break flow, to the pattern, has a definite advantage if the attack is continuous.

Nonflexible patterns do not have an occasional option, but on the whole the individual skills of the players must be subjugated to the whims of the motion. The coach certainly has a real handle on offensive control. It forces the players to have, and to use, the specific motion skills, or fail to get any benefit from grooving the action into the tight team motion. It asks all the players to have equal abilities in the running of the motion.

In a pattern that is flexible (with the team motion giving each player an opportunity to contribute according to his skill efficiency), the skill improvement of your individual players will show immediately. Such a pattern has enough organization to keep all five players in contact with the movements of each player's known relationships.

The attack is open enough for any player to take advantage of the first defensive mistake. This is a different approach from the passing up of an open inside lane to make three more dribbles, or passes, when moving through the motion three or four times.

High school players may well be mechanical in the early stages of their development, but you cannot allow them to stay mechanical and expect them to win the ultimate championship. You must teach savvy. Savvy is one of the byproducts of this entire offensive system. It helps you to develop thinking ball players.

From basic break to the Go Behind

All the offensive patterns will begin from the 1-2-2 set because that is the alignment with which the secondary break ends. Diagram 7-9 displays the famous Go Behind offense. Player 3 has passed to player 2 but player 2 could not get an advantage on the initial thrust of the primary break. Player 3 goes behind player 2 to get the pass from him. Player 1, meanwhile, has come into the lane area to help player 5 set a double screen. After player 2 hands the ball off to player 3, he breaks around the screen set by player 4. If X2 goes behind player 4, player 2 steps out high for a pass from player 3 and a jump shot. Players 1, 4, and 5 hit the offensive boards. If X2 tries to follow player 2 over 4's screen, player 2 breaks hard to the basket for a pass and a lay-up. If none of this materializes, players 4 and 3 work a two-man game. Player 4 sets the screen for player 3 to drive over the top, and 4 rolls to the basket. If X3 tries to prevent player 3 from driving over the top, he has a baseline drive for a lay-up. Player 3 can pass to player 4 on his roll to the basket, or 3 can pass to 2 coming around the double screen being set by players 1 and 5. Player 2 can read his defensive coverage as he goes around the double screen. If the defender stays to help on the screen-and-roll by players 3 and 4, player 2 has the jump shot behind the double screen. If X2 goes over the top of the double screen, player 2 can come back

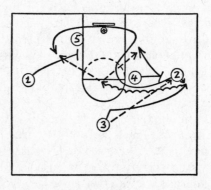

Diagram 7-9

baseline for a lay-up. If X2 trails player 2 around the double screen, player 2 can continue on around it for the pass from player 3 and the jump shot or lay-up. From this positioning you could reset or you could go immediately into a motion game, or move into another famous pattern like the Wheel.

From fast break to the Baseline Shuffle

Coach Pete Newell used this half-court offense in 1959 to win the NCAA Championships. It is still widely used today. Player 3 drives toward one elbow of the free-throw line (Diagram 7-10). The opposite big man, player 5 in Diagram 7-10, pops out as far as he has to in order to

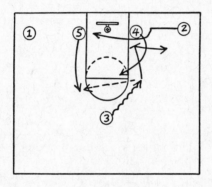

Diagram 7-10

get the pass from player 3. If overplayed too hard, player 5 can show player 3 the fist and race backdoor for the lay-up. When player 2 sees player 3 pass to player 5, he uses the screen set by player 4 and breaks along the baseline for a pass from 5 and the lay-up. Meanwhile player 3 has screened for player 4, who pops high near the elbow for a pass from 5 and the possible jumper. If player 4 is played too tightly, he can drive for the lay-up. If player 4 is overplayed prior to receiving the pass from player 5, he can show the fist and go backdoor for the lay-up. Now the offense is set to run from the other side.

Diagram 7-11 shows the offense coming from the new positions, thereby making it a shuffle offense. When player 5 passes to player 4, player 1 cuts off of player 2's baseline screen. A pass from player 4 to player 1 would get a lay-up. Meanwhile player 5 has set a screen for

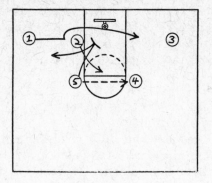

Diagram 7-11

player 2. Player 2 pops up to the elbow with the same options that player 4 had previously. Now the offense is set again on the right side. By continuing the offense from one side of the court to the other, you are running the baseline shuffle.

From fast break to the Wheel

The Wheel offense was made famous for many years by Garland Pinholster while at Oglethorpe University. Many high school and college teams still run this highly disciplined shuffle offense.

Diagram 7-12 shows the initial double post set. Nothing develops for player 2 so player 4 goes to screen for player 5, ending the secondary break. Player 4 rolls back to high post. Player 2 passes to player 3, and players 4 and 5 slide together to set a double screen for player 2. Player 3 passes to player 1. If player 1 is overplayed, he should show the fist and go backdoor. When player 2 sees player 1 receive the pass, he breaks off of the double screen for a pass from player 1 and the lay-up. Player 2 reads his defensive coverage. If X2 is overplaying him high, player 2 should step toward his opponent, then dart on the baseline side of the double screen. If X2 is playing the baseline side of player 2, he should step toward X2 and break over the top of the double screen. After player 3 passes to player 1, he goes down to set a screen on players 4 and 5. Player 5 breaks around the double screen set by players 4 and 3 for a jump shot near the elbow. Player 4, meanwhile, goes to the point to receive the reverse pass from player 1. Player 3, after setting his screen for players 4 and 5, moves out to a wing position.

Diagram 7-13 shows the new positions of the players after they have run one side of the Wheel offense. Player 1 passes to player 4 who looks to feed player 3. Player 3 has the same options as player 1 had initially. Players 5 and 2 get ready to set the double screen. Player 1, after he

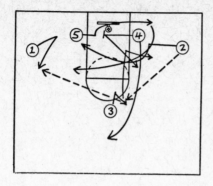

Diagram 7-12

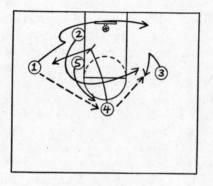

Diagram 7-13

passes to player 4, reads player 4's pass to player 3. This cues player 1 to read his man and break off the double screen. The Wheel offense is now beginning on the other side of the floor.

From fast break to UCLA Power offense

Diagram 7-14 displays the move which gets the fast break into the UCLA Power offense. Player 3 advances the ball down the floor and passes to player 2. Player 2 tries to score off of the primary break, but he is unsuccessful. Player 3 could meanwhile have gone and screened for player 1 if that is your wish. Diagram 7-14 shows player 3 staying at the point while player 2 checks inside to low post player 4 as you would have him do in the secondary break. After a pass back to player 3, the UCLA Power offense begins. Player 3 can pass to either player 2 or 1. Player 3

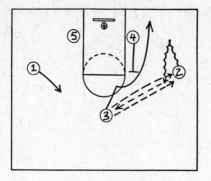

Diagram 7-14

reads his defender cutting off of player 4 at the high post. If **X3** covers ball side, player 3 breaks off player 4 on the basket side. If **X3** covers the middle of the court, player 3 cuts off player 4 on the ball side. After player 3 cuts off player 4, player 4 steps outside to receive a pass from player 2. If player 4 is overplayed, he can give the fist signal and go backdoor. Or player 4 can be taught to screen down for 5, and players 4 and 5 exchange duties. In Diagram 7-15 player 4 has received the pass from player 2. Player 4 now checks player 5 on his post-up move in the middle. If X5 overplays, the lob pass gets a lay-up. If X5 allows the direct pass to 5, player 5 has a power move for a possible 3-point play. If X5 covers player 5 well, player 4 can pass to player 1 who might be able to hit 5 inside, especially if player 5 has been taught to hold his perfect position on X5.

Meanwhile, when player 2 passed to player 4, 2 set a screen on player 3. Player 3 now takes a step or so toward the basket, setting up X3.

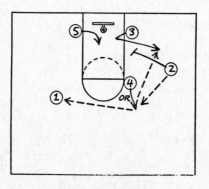

Diagram 7-15

Player 3 breaks around the screen set by player 2. Player 4 can pass inside to 2 or he can pass to player 3. Player 3 now has an individual move he can use, or 3 can pass in to player 2 posting up. After a second or so, player 2 can screen for player 5 who breaks off player 2's screen and posts up on the big block.

All these famous offenses were shown from a 1-2-2 alignment. Books have been written on the offenses. All of them can be run from a two-guard front if that is your preference. Just purchase one of the books and get the offense from a two-guard front. The front you run from should correspond with the ending of your secondary break. Also, these famous offenses have many more options to their basic patterns. And they have several interchangeable patterns.

Zone offenses

Fast passing on the perimeter, and well-timed inside motion, are the keys to penetrating the zone. A quick outside penetration of the zone's front line, with inside players flashing into the open passing lanes, creates problems for the zone. The zone generally has the shifting ability to keep up with a medium passing tempo.

Players attacking the zone should be working at all times for ballside position, which forces the zone to overshift. Quick reverse moves create open passing lanes to the inside if the passing team is ready to take instant advantage.

The passing tempo is vitally important to get a step advantage. It is also important to force the zone to make three or four moves that will create the zone overshift or a move to unfamiliar coverages.

The zone is forced to anticipate the pass motion, which allows the fake passing to open up the passing lanes. This is necessary to get a good shot.

A long fake will throw the defenders out of the passing lanes. A team that can bounce-pass quickly and accurately with no telegraphing will beat a zone defense.

Screening a front-line zone player, or a back line player, is important. It is a move that helps neutralize zone players' ability to pressure a shot or force the pass in their zone area. The single dribble drive at an open slot between two zone defenders forces them to weaken lanes on either side of the dribbler. The dribbler needs to be quick with the stop-and-pass to his teammate, who might be able to exploit the lane opening.

The fast break team works for at least 75 shots a game. The zone battles to hold the shot number in the 50s. Passing will be a big key to get the break's 75 shots. Time is vitally important to you in getting your shots. You must have patience to get the good shot without letting the zone dictate how long you have to take to get it.

Zone defenders play with their hands high, and they want the passes you throw to be in that same plane. If you are using the overhead pass, be sure to use a continuous faking motion. The overhead passer should develop the skill of quickly pulling the ball down while employing a front pivot move, to protect the ball against expanded pressure tactics. The overhead pass should be quick with a fast release. Fake to low passing lanes ahead of your overhead passing move.

The bounce pass has become the most important weapon for cracking the zone. The bounce counters the zone's hands-up policy. Work on it to develop speed in getting the ball to your inside teammates. A quick single move, or two-dribble move, that covers 10 to 20 feet is another important skill which helps to defeat the zone. Flashing this distance is like having a sixth player on the floor. Many high school players gain very little distance with the single dribble.

An ever-present rule: every player should meet all passes. Even a jump move is better than being caught standing. The two-handed chest pass follow-through should be cut short after the passer becomes accurate. The accurate, quick release keeps the zone defense's hands from tagging or intercepting passes.

Keep your eyes down, watching the feet and hands of your teammate before passing. Zone players read the passer's eyes.

Your inside motion should be quick and on time. Many passing attacks spend half the time being late, with the ball reversing away. This forces the inside attackers to try to catch up with the ball. Teach the inside tempo to stay up with the pass attack. Keep moving. Don't move across the zone and get caught standing.

Many high school players have a tendency to stand after they pass the ball. Such a player could be the most dangerous man on the court if, instead of standing, he would execute flash moves after passing. Zone defenses love the standing offensive player.

Outside perimeter passers should work hard on moves after they execute the pass. Use hard-attack fakes to pressure the zone defense back out of the lanes. Always execute a quick release away from the defender when a teammate is ready to pass.

Fast breaking the zone defense is an easy way to defeat it. After going into the secondary break and the set offense, you need to keep in mind the above coaching points. The following is a good summary:

1. The ball should be passed in quickly after an opponent makes a shot and brought up the floor fast to keep on the heels of the retreating zone. You have the opportunity to attack and cut through the zone before the zone

forms. Your rebounders want to be going to the board as your teammate takes a shot. It is almost impossible for zone defenders to block off their defensive boards, especially when in transition.

2. Keep the ball moving from side to side as you race up the floor and after you have gone into your secondary break and beyond.

3. All the attack players should be ready to cut over the top of retreating zone players. Do not go behind unless there is a lot of room for the pass to get through or over.

4. Make use of the dribble drive. Zones must adjust leaving the lanes beside the drive open.

5. Learn the distinction between holding up the shot and attacking all the way.

6. Backline attackers should recognize they have inside positions on the high zone defenders, and they should stay strong on the boards. Any missed shot will become a lay-up.

7. Work hard on being able to pass from the point into the high post area.

8. Shoot on receiving a pass. Don't give the zone time to recover and stop your shot because of faulty footwork.

From fast break into the Boston College Overload

This offense was created by Dr. Tom Davis when he was at Boston College. Since its creation, many coaches have adopted it and many have changed it somewhat to fit their particular personnel.

Diagram 7-16 shows how the fast break goes to the secondary break and on into the Boston College Overload. In Diagram 7-16, the wing player opposite the entry pass for the secondary break darts out along

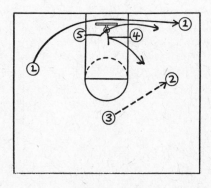

Diagram 7-16

the baseline and into the corner. You could easily adjust this by requiring that player 3 break into the strongside corner.

Player 2 has immediate shot options available (Diagram 7-16). Player 2 can pass inside to player 4 at high post or inside to player 5 at the low post. A pass to the high post requires that the low post player roll across the lane. A pass to the low post requires that the high post player break down the lane for a pass or proper rebound position.

Player 2 could pass to player 1 in the corner. When the pass goes to player 1 (especially if player 2 has driven toward the basket) he usually has an easy baseline shot. Player 1 could check the high post and low post for possible passes there. Any pass into either high or low post activates the above rules.

Player 2 could reverse the pass to player 3. When that happens the players change sides and attack from the opposite side of the court (Diagram 7-17). The post men, players 4 and 5, did not stay still, looking for the passes from players 2 or 1. They rolled. This roll puts player 5 in perfect position to break along the elbow and receive the pass from player 3. Player 1 raced along the baseline. Player 4 cut along the baseline after player 1, posting his man up on the low block. Player 5 passed inside the corner to player 1 and broke through the high post area of the zone. Player 2 comes across the high post area to the position vacated by player 4. But if player 1 can get the pass inside to player 2, he can dump the ball down to either players 5 or 4 for lay-ups. If player 2 has the jumper, both players 5 and 4 have perfect inside rebounding position. The zone offense can keep swinging from side to side until an opening develops. This zone offense works equally well against all zone defenses.

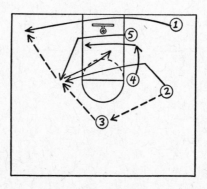

Diagram 7-17

From fast break to the Marquette Zone offense

Diagram 7-18 displays the method of going from fast break to secondary phase to the Marquette Zone offense. It too works equally well against all zone defenses.

After going to low post positions for the secondary break, players 4 and 5 move back up to medium post position for the Marquette Zone Offense (Diagram 7-18). Player 3 becomes the swing man, running the baseline against all zones, creating an overload to whichever side he cuts. Player 1 tries to feed post player 5. If this is not available and player 3 cuts to the opposite side, player 1 will dribble toward the middle of the court and swing the ball to player 2. Player 2 can penetrate and dish off to player 3 for the shot. Player 2 can pass inside to post player 4. Post players 4 and 5 can exchange positions by rolling or screening. Player 3 can again run the baseline to the weak side or he can stay strong side. Player 2 can pass back to player 1, who has the same options as he receives the ball as player 2 had on the opposite side. If player 3 stayed on the weak side, a pass cross-court and a screen by the low post player usually gets an easy shot. This type of passing and movement continues until the offense gets the shot it wants.

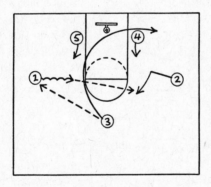

Diagram 7-18

A single movement down court

Diagrams 7-19, 7-20, and 7-21 show a simple single movement down court which takes the offense through the primary break into the secondary break into the set offense. And it all occurs without any resetting.

Diagram 7-19 depicts the basic fast break, with the ball being outletted to player 2 who passes inside to player 3 in the middle lane. Player 3 passes to player 1 on the fly pattern. Player 1 passes back to player 3. Player 3 dribbles a step or so before passing to player 2. Now we are in the final phase of the primary break.

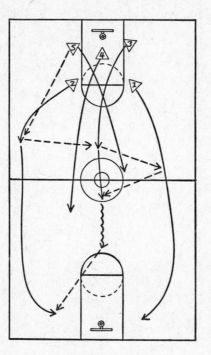

Diagram 7-19

Diagram 7-20 shows that player 2 did not get the driving lay-up or the jump shot off the primary break. So the secondary break began immediately. Player 2 has all the options previously described for post players 4 and 5 on their posting-up inside and screen-and-roll technique.

Nothing materialized from the secondary break. The offense is now in a position to run the Wheel, the Triple Post against the man-to-man, pass to player 5 running the baseline or inside to player 4 at high post, or reverse-pass to player 3 and we are running our zone offense. Player 1 could have run the baseline and you would have the Boston College Zone Offense (Diagram 7-21).

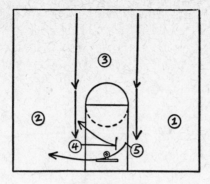

Diagram 7-20

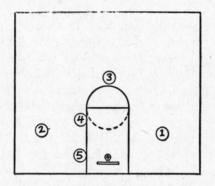

Diagram 7-21

SECRETS OF USING
YOUR FAST BREAK
FROM SPECIAL SITUATIONS

8

First you want to establish your basic fast break with options, rebound moves, and variations. Then your fast break offense can be applied to every floor situation. Your team can run the same cuts whether the ball is recovered from a made basket, a missed free throw, a center tip, or an out-of-bounds play. The offensive fast break also attacks the full-court zone presses.

Such simplicity should make it easy for the fast break team to fill the running and passing lanes at the instant of ball recovery. Nothing new has been added: the offense, already learned, has been expanded to take advantage of each turn-over, missed shot, made basket, or free throw; to defense forced errors, out-of-bounds, held balls, steals, traps; and to cope with the full-court zone pressure defenses. One of the beauties of this fast break system is it can be used in all special situations.

Secrets of the Fast Break from Made Shots

The same basic pattern is available after shots are made from the field or from the free-throw line. You merely assign player 5 the job of always inbounding the ball. Player 2 has the assignment of getting open to receive the inbounds pass. Player 1 always runs his fly pattern. Player 3 runs his ordinary route down the middle lane. Player 3 has the option of cutting outside in the left side lane, buttonhooking back to the ball, or timing his cut down the middle so he can receive the pass from player 2. But player 4 may have to make an adjustment in his regular route.

Player 4, as shown in Diagram 8-1, makes an adjustment when Player 2 is face-guarded or double-teamed or short-stopped. Some opponents try this strategy, hoping to disrupt the throw-in to player 2. Player 4 comes back to get the inbounds pass from player 5. This is player 4's buttonhook move, but 4 might have to do some cutting from one lane to another to free himself. After player 4 receives the inbounds pass, player 2 breaks down court, leaving his defenders behind. Frequently 2 is wide open when he runs this fly pattern, as he would have run when the outlet pass was being defensed. Player 2 now has all the options of the basic break available.

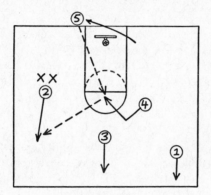

Diagram 8-1

Player 4 merely performed one of his basic break options. Player 3, in effect, cleared the middle lane with a fly pattern and 4 responded by coming back to the ball.

In case there is no pressure on player 2 trying to get the inbounds pass, it is easy for player 5 to get the ball and toss it inbounds to player 2. You can designate a spot for this pass, or you can leave it to player 5 to find player 2 quickly. Player 1 has filled his right lane, and a lay-up can result by player 2 quickly hitting player 1. Player 3 had an option of going down the middle or going to the sideline. Player 2 can frequently hit player 3, who is finding the open lane. Player 2 then fills the lane which is not occupied by player 3. Player 4 runs hard down the middle lane, preparing to rebound the missed shot by either player 3 or 1 or preparing to commence the secondary phase of the fast break.

Often it is possible to score within seconds after your opponents have scored. To successfully accomplish this, player 5 must hurriedly get the ball and move it inbounds. Player 5 can even hit player 1 or 3 with a baseball pass. Teammates of player 5 can grab the ball out of the net and pass outside to him. Player 5 inbounds and goes off the fast break.

Secrets of the Fast Break from the Free-Throw Line

The free-throw situation offers an opportunity to develop a quick break up the floor from either the made or the missed free throw. The break move works equally well against a team that delays retreating by quickly hurrying to press positions. Many teams will press after made free throws.

Diagram 8-2 illustrates one way to get the break started after a made free throw. You can also use this method to always run your fast break after made baskets. The missed free throw can also use the same techniques.

Players 4 and 5 take the board positions with players 1 and 3 taking the third positions. Player 1 steps in and screens the shooter from the ball. Player 3, after going to the boards, cuts down the middle lane as he does in all the fast break situations. Player 2 flashes from his center court position to the long outlet pass receiving position to receive rebounder 5's out-of-bounds pass. Player 2 passes to player 3 who is cutting down the center lane.

Player 1, after the screen, cuts quickly to take over the side lane and runs his fly pattern. Player 2 streaks down the left side lane to get ahead of the center lane cutter, player 3. Player 3 passes off to weakside player 1, who passes back to 3, who passes to 2. Or player 2 could dribble to the top of the key, ready to pass to the open player. All the options of the basic break are available, whether the free throw is made or missed.

If the free throw is missed, player 2 would go to the side of the rebound for the long outlet pass. Player 1 would screen and have to

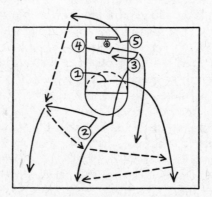

Diagram 8-2

make a necessary adjustment. Player 1 would go on his fly pattern opposite the side of the rebound. If the ball were rebounded down the middle, you could designate which side for players 2 and 1 to run their routes. The remainder of the fast break is the same.

Secrets of the Fast Break from Sideline Out-of-Bounds

When your team is being pressured full court on out-of-bounds plays, your regular fast break options are available. Diagram 8-3 shows player 5 screening for player 2, and player 4 screening for player 1. Player 1 runs his fly pattern after accepting the screen. If player 3 hits player 2, who has accepted the screen from player 5, player 3 quickly fills the middle lane and the break is off and running. Of course, player 2 could impel player 3 to change lanes by dribbling to the middle lane. Player 3 could inbounds to player 5, and the break looks like a rebound break. Player 5 can outlet pass to player 2, who comes back to the ball. Player 2 can hit 3 in the middle lane cut, throw to player 1 on the fly, or hit player 4 after player 3 clears the middle lane of defenders. These are the moves of the basic break.

After the ball is inbounded, all the options of the basic break are available. And if you wish to switch to another variation, like the sideline break, those, too, are available. One of the beauties of the fast break system is its versatility: it works against free throws, baskets, out-of-bounds, tips, and full-court zone and man-to-man pressure. You only have one offense to teach. You can teach it in detail. You can drill it until it is instinctive. And you run it against all full-court defensive roadblocks.

Diagrams 8-4 and 8-5 reveal a sideline out-of-bounds play against man-to-man defense in your own offensive end of the court. So the final

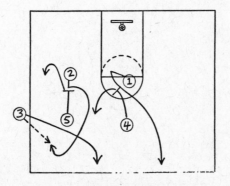

Diagram 8-3

phase of the fast break offense can be put to use on out-of-bounds plays, when pressured, on the offensive end of the court.

Player 1 takes the ball out-of-bounds. Player 5 screens for player 3 and player 2. If possible you want the ball inbounded to player 3 (Diagram 8-4). After inbounding the ball, player 4 sets a blind back-pick for player 1 to run his man into. Player 5, meanwhile, has screened for player 2. Player 4 on his roll-back to low post position also sets a moving screen for player 2. Player 3 begins his dribble toward the middle of the court.

Diagram 8-5 continues the play begun in Diagram 8-4. Player 3 is dribbling toward the middle of the court while looking for scoring opportunities. Player 3 could have hit player 1 if he was free after using player 4's screen. Player 3 could have hit player 4 on his roll-back toward low post position. If none of that developed, player 3 can pass to either player 2 or player 1 and begin the secondary phase of the fast break.

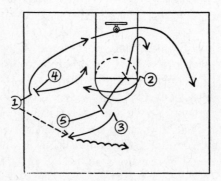

Diagram 8-4

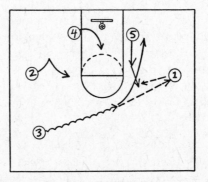

Diagram 8-5

Secrets of the Fast Break from Held Ball Tips

There are several varieties of tips that can be used in which the results are the same as the basic break: The running lanes and the passing options are the same. One set with player 3 tipping and one set without player 3 tipping will be presented. Another wide-open tip play will also be shown. From these tip plays, you can easily see how you can work up one to fit your material yet stay with the passing and running options of the basic break.

Diagram 8-6 shows a held ball play without your primary player, player 3, tipping. The two wings stationed at the sides of the tip will move in tighter if there is any question about making the tip to player 3. Even if the tip goes back to player 5, the break is still on. A tip back to player 5 corresponds to player 5 getting a rebound, outlet passing to

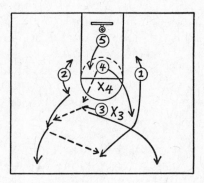

Diagram 8-6

player 2, etc. in the basic break. A signal or a stance will tell player 3 which way to move to get the tip. All eyes are watching the tipping hands go up for the ball. Players 1 and 2 cut down their lanes as they see the ball tipped. Player 5 is the safety who gets possession if the ball is tipped back or if your team loses the tip. Tipping a ball back, however, is a dangerous strategy in this area. Player 4 trails player 3 cutting down the middle lane on the tip side, while the tip safety player 5 cuts down away from the tip after the ball has been cleared. As you can see, the tip ends in the regular cuts of the basic break. The variations are also available.

Diagram 8-7 illustrates a held ball set with player 3 tipping. If player 3 tips back to player 5, 3 races up the center lane, letting player 4 fill in for the vacated area. But in Diagram 8-7, player 3 tips to player 1. Player 3 fills the opposite outside lane while player 2 occupies the middle lane.

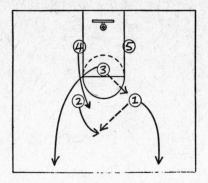

Diagram 8-7

If player 3 had tipped to player 2, player 1 would have taken the middle lane and player 3 the right side lane.

Diagram 8-8 shows a tip play if you are sure of the tip and if you want to force the opposition to make adjustments. Player 4 could tip to either players 1 or 2 and let player 3 go on a fly. The opposite sideline player would take the middle lane. Or player 2 could dribble to the middle lane. The sideline variation is easily run by having player 2 hit player 3 and cut to the middle lane.

A simple variation to this tip play would have the tip go to player 3 and players 1 and 2 both run fly patterns.

These tip sequences were shown from the defensive end of the court. They work just as well at the center court tip. Of course, no fast break is available if you are at your offensive end. All the options of the basic break are available; and all the variations can be considered. Nothing new must be learned.

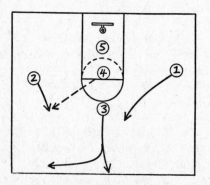

Diagram 8-8

Secrets of the Fast Break Against the Full-Court Press

A great deal of practice time will be saved if you work your fast break variations as a counter to the full-court press. The press down court actually sets up the fast break opportunities. The quick transition to offense is important. Designate one player as an out-of-bounds passer; the same one should be used against the press as the one who throws the ball in against made baskets. If other teammates are closer to the ball, tap or pass the ball quickly to this designated out-of-bounds passer. Be sure to train at least one more out-of-bounds passer in the starting five and one substitute. The one trained should carry the ball high on his shoulder, cocked to pass as he jumps out-of-bounds. He should be one of your best passers who is a large, tall man. These type passers should be big men because they are usually closer to the basket when your opponents score. Also, they can see over any big defensive player stationed on them. You must train this out-of-bounds passer to break up the middle or receive a return pass from the wing and reverse the ball, or be able to put it on the floor for at least one dribble.

Your three fast-break frontal lane players move into their positions, about two steps back of the key and behind the defensive press's front line. They should fake a starting motion away from either the passing lane or the cutting lanes to be used. This can be called "faking the defender away from the passing or running lane." Cutters start their motion just before the out-of-bounds passer gets set to pass. They break hard for an open lane before moving back to the ball.

Some coaches use a fake-break up court, then back toward the passer, to open the passing lane. This vertical start-stop-and-start motion does not clear the pass receiver as well as the cuts from one passing lane to another. By cutting a little vertically but much more horizontally, passing lanes against zone presses open up for a fast break attack.

This type of motion forces defenders to cover from sideline to sideline. By cutting fast and passing quickly to the outside shoulder of the receiver, defenders who intercept passes frequently continue on out-of-bounds. The vertical interception, however, goes directly toward the opponents' basket. Vertical interceptions usually end in an easy fast break basket for your opponents.

Several different but very similar attacks against full court pressure are presented. They all end with the basic break's running and passing lanes. Some are more complicated; some are simple. It is your choice. The first is the simplest. It is where the players usually have raced to begin the break after a made basket (Diagram 8-9). Player 5 can pass to either player 4 or player 2. Either of these two players can continue the basic fast break. Player 5 would want to make a diagonal cut up the sideline that he threw the ball into. This cut is extremely difficult for either the box or diamond zone press to stop.

Diagram 8-9 displays player 5 passing in to player 4 or player 2. Player 5 breaks up the sideline he passed to, let's say player 2. Player 3, meanwhile, has cut back toward the ball in the middle lane. A pass from player 2 to player 3 and out to the other side, player 1, results in the press being broken. All players run their straight line fast break. Most of the time, press breaking is not that simple. But player 5's cut cannot be stopped by any zone press. A pass from player 2 to player 5 cannot be covered or defensed by any of the major zone presses. Player 5 can dribble one dribble to maintain balance and be sure he does not run over a defender. Player 3 breaks at a diagonal to receive a pass from player 5. Player 2 has broken up the center lane. Usually player 3 and player 1 have a 2-on-1 break. But if the 2-on-1 break is not present, the lanes are filled to end the primary break and go directly to the secondary phase.

Diagram 8-10 shows player 5's inbound passing options. Player 5 passes to either players 1, 2, or 3, your best ball handlers. This attack is a little more complicated than the one presented in Diagram 8-9. Once the ball is passed inbounds, player 4 goes on his fly pattern, taking the place of player 1. You do this because you have a player 1 who is more capable of breaking the press. If player 1 hits player 3, 1 races on his middle cut. If player 3 or player 2 receive the inbounds pass, player 1 races on his middle cut. If player 2 should pass to 1, player 2 races on a middle cut.

If you prefer to stay with the same players making the same basic break cuts, all you have to do is change the numbers. For example, change player 4 to player 1 and player 1 to player 4 and you have the basic break.

Diagram 8-11 illustrates the quick reverse off the same positions and motions. Player 2 pulls to the right side lane as he sees the pass start to player 4. Player 4 can receive the pass from player 5 from out-of-bounds, or player 1 can call the reverse by passing to player 4.

These last two diagrams have the same motion that is evident in the basic break. The sideline series is also available as a variation. Instead of passing and cutting down the middle lane, the passer cuts to a side lane.

High school teams have a tendency to go to spots and just stand. It is easy to pick off passes that are thrown to standing targets. The front line must have good motion and should mix up the sideline and ball fake moves, then go hard to meet the pass. Your out-of-bounds passer should be seeing three open lanes with his teammates moving toward the ball. He should pass first to the side lane cutter to force the press to shift. Also, he should try hard to hit the center man or the second lane filler. The fast break starts from either lane entry.

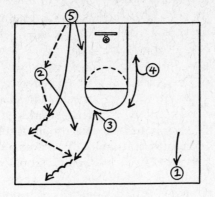

Diagram 8-9

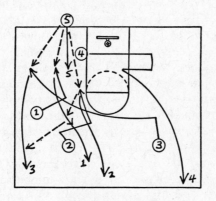

Diagram 8-10

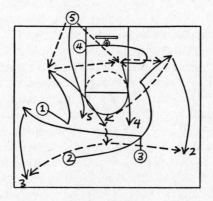

Diagram 8-11

Be sure to eliminate the fast-break front line running away from the opponent's made basket, which forces the guards to come from the perimeter to put the ball into play. The nearest front liner should at least tap the ball or hand it to the out-of-bounds passer. Don't give the press any time to set up. Move the ball to player 5 immediately after the score. And get the pass inbounds and the break underway just as quickly.

Diagram 8-12 demonstrates a box out-of-bounds pattern which results in the same fast break defeating a full-court zone press. Success depends on quick motion and short passes. Every player who receives a pass should immediately use up-court spread vision. He fakes before passing using quick passing judgment.

Player 5 has four immediate pass opportunities from out-of-bounds. Player 1 on the left side lane, players 2 or 3 in the center lane, and player 4 on the reverse are four primary receivers. The pass may go directly to player 3. Player 2 cuts for the right side lane, with player 3 passing to player 1 cutting down the left side lane. Player 2 cuts back toward the right side lane. Player 5 may pass to player 4, with player 3 cutting to the right side lane. Player 4 may pass to player 2 or player 3. Player 5 comes in fast, ready for any back-pass and to act as safety if there is a steal. Players 3 and 2 may option to dribble-cut to the head of the key. The player who receives the pass after crossing the ten-second line will dribble if the passing lanes are closed. At any time the attack may switch from the basic straight line fast break to the sideline and dribble variations.

Diagram 8-13 offers a clockwise motion counter-move that can be used to defeat a press. The three players on the front line set up just above the head of the key and start in motion as the out-of-bounds passer, player 5, gets to his out-of-bounds position. Speed is very important. Player 5 should grab the ball as it clears the bottom of the net. Player 1 fakes the basic sideline fast break move, then comes to meet the pass. If he does not receive the ball, he continues away under the basket ready to fill any lane, or to come back for a pass. Player 3 fakes down, then cuts to the sideline and takes player 1's fast break position to receive the outlet pass. Player 4 cuts away across the key ready to come back to the ball, or to be the second center lane cutter. Player 2 fakes his fast break basic move then races to the center lane to receive the inbounds pass. Players 2 and 4 will fill the open lane or fake the second cutter move with player 5 coming up court behind the break to act as a safety until the break nears the head of the key. He then moves through for a rebound, post-up position, or begins the secondary break.

When player 5 hits player 3, he passes to the center lane cutter, player 2. Player 2 hits player 3 on his cut, and the break is on. If player 5 passes to player 4, the attack reverses as player 4 passes to the side lane cutter, player 1, who passes to the center lane cutter, player 2. Player 4 steps inside in position to receive a pass if the play is stalled.

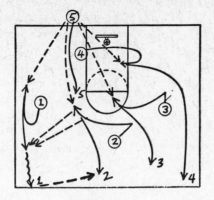

Diagram 8-12

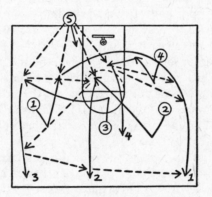

Diagram 8-13

Sometimes the defense will call a quick time-out after they have scored. When play resumes, the defense will use face-guard or denial tactics. You could respond with screens. Once you inbounds the ball, your fast break attack can still be in operation. Diagram 8-14 shows a stick set to inbounds the ball. This could be your only press offense or it could be a press offense you use against denial pressure.

You could have three different set positions. The first set position could be just inside the free-throw line; the second could be just ahead of the key; and the third could be inside the free-throw line and circle. With the full court press anchored close to the baseline, one of the longer positions would be best. Against three-quarter presses, the second positioning would be the best.

Player 5 grabs the ball and goes out-of-bounds to a position about halfway to the sideline. The time-out is called. When you set your of-

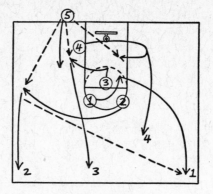

Diagram 8-14

fense back up, you should remind player 5 to begin at a different position and race to the spot halfway to the sideline.

Player 4 cuts across the key near the baseline ready to come back for a safety valve pass if the other lanes are closed. Player 4 will break down court as a second center lane cutter. Player 3, the point of the triangle, cuts down between players 1 and 2 and fills the center lane as a first cutter. Players 1 and 2 crisscross and break for the sidelines. They can develop signals to change the lane patterns for each player. Players 1 and 2 may not cross, but instead break out to each player's positions near the sidelines.

Player 3 on signal may cut to the outlet area and receive the entry pass from player 5. Players 3 and 4 could exchange lane assignments which might help to confuse a particular press.

The entry pass can be to either players 3, 2, or 4 with a possible long pass to player 1. If player 3 is hit, he can pass to player 2, as shown in Diagram 8-14, or he can pass back to player 4 and reverse the ball to player 1 coming back toward the pass. Player 3 can dribble up the center lane. If the pass comes in to player 2, player 3 would break up the center lane for a pass from player 2. Player 4 would follow player 3 in case 3 would have to clear the defense out of the center lane. Player 2 could dribble or pass to player 3 or 4, or he could throw the long fly pattern to player 1.

Six different, but highly similar, attacks against full-court presses have been presented. You would never want to use all six. One or two would suffice. You know your team personnel and the difficulty they will have against presses for any one year.

All the press offenses end in the basic break. With a little imagination, you could switch the basic break to the sideline variation or the dribble variation.

You could change the numbers in the diagrams to correspond to the skills of the players you have on hand. Numbers have been purposely changed in different orders in a few of the diagrams so you could realize you do not have to have the same center cutter as we propose. If your material dictates that player 4, for example, can handle the ball going up the center lane but player 3 could not, you change the numbers on the diagrams and you have a perfect full-court press offense. The beauty of it all is you don't have to teach a different full-court press attack; you just expand the options of your fast break attack.

Looking Back

If we had made our excessive claims prior to your reading this book, you would not have believed them. We purposely withheld our claims until after you had seen the movements of this transition offense. We waited until you had seen the evidence.

It is undeniably simple.

It can be run from a patterned, highly structured system. Half of the coaches in the world are very structured.

It can be run by teaching savvy and allowing the player to make choices which keep the break alive and moving. The other half of the world's coaches are in this category.

It can be taught by rules—guidelines which must be obeyed. These rules are flexible enough to allow lane changing and passing options.

It can become completely freelance.

It cannot be stopped by defensive roadblocks because you have more options ahead of the ball than there can possibly be defenders.

It can be coupled with other types of fast breaks: the sideline fast break variation, for example.

At the end of the primary break, there are innumerable opportunities to score.

Should the primary break fail, there exists a secondary break which has an inordinate number of scoring opportunities.

And if the secondary break fails, you are set for beginning your half-court attack without allowing the defense a moment's reset time, without allowing them a rest.

The most beautiful feature of the transitional offense, besides its simplicity, is that it can be run from made-and-missed shots, made-and-missed free throws, tips, out-of-bounds, turnovers, and against full-court presses. That allows you to teach the basic break in greater detail, knowing you can use it in all kinds of situations. Think of the practice time you will save.

INDEX